MY SOUL TO HIS SPIRIT:

*SOULFUL EXPRESSIONS FROM
BLACK DAUGHTERS TO THEIR FATHERS*

EDITED BY
MELDA BEATY

SoulDictates Publishing
Illinois

Published by:
SoulDictates Publishing
P.O. Box 587926
Alsip, Illinois 60803-7926

www.mysoultohisspirit.com

ISBN 0-9765624-1-3

Library of Congress Control Number 2005900343

Designed by Lynnette L. Galloway

Printed in the United States of America

First Edition: May 2005

For black daughters everywhere,
And in loving memory of my aunt and soror
Dr. Patricia Potts.
Your influence in my life is forever my muse.

Contents

Acknowledgments ix

Introduction: An Epiphany Melda Beaty 1

CHAPTER I
LOVING: DADDY'S GIRL 8

A Loving Dad	Adina Jordan Andrews	10
Staying Afloat: Because of Him	Michelle D. Parrish	14
Papi Was a Dancing Man	Avotcja	15
Loving Daddy	Suzetta M. Perkins	17
Daddy's Eyes	Tauheedah Shakoor-Strong	19
Daddy's Little Girl	Gabriella Miller	22
The Essence of Manhood	Tedella Gowans	24
The First Man to Love Me: James Bernice Brown	Angela D. Gittens	26
Lessons from My Father	Pamela Gilmore	28
My Husband Got a Job on His Hands	Kotanya K. Kimbrough	30
Giant Revealed: For Dad	Sandra Morris	32
A Father's Lesson by Example	Denise L. Johnson	33
Daddy's Hardworking Hands	Virginia K. Lee	35
Precious Lord		36
Surely He Knows This	Julie Amari-Bandele	37
Dancing on Daddy's Feet	Akua Lezli Hope	38
A Simple Gift	Imani Powell	39

CHAPTER II
DISTANT: EVERY ONCE IN AWHILE 42

Tears for Fears	Tina Smith Walker	44
A Childhood Stream of Consciousness	Kathyrn Buford	46
hock daddy	Barbara Lewis	49
Jailbird's Wing: Poems for My Father	Meredith Bloedorn	50
The Father I Now Know	Chante` Bowns	54
Ceremonies	Sharon R. Amos	56
Reckoning	Raquel Rivera	57
Estrangement	Linda Susan Jackson	59
A Birthday Card from My Father	Opal Palmer Adisa	60

Contents

CHAPTER III
ABANDONED: ONE DAY HE WAS GONE 66

Faith[1]	Niama Williams	68
An Open Letter to My Dad	J. Victoria Sanders	71
Fear #2	Michelle R. Smith	75
Superhero	Mary Ruth Theodos	76
Erasing the Past Pain with a Smile	Nesheba Kittling	79
To Compare My Love to My Mother's	Gabrielle Lee	80
Missing in Action	Sandra Morris	82
Blurred Images	Toya Lay	83
Unresolved	Pam Osbey	85
Daddy's Little Girl	Kieshawn Middleton	87
Fruit of Corrupt Seed	Johannas Williams	88
Dinner at My Father's House, December 2000	Opal Palmer Adisa	93

CHAPTER IV
NON-EXISTENT: COULD PASS ME ON THE STREET 98

Letters to Daddy	Samaiya Ewing	100
Lost but Never Found	Mae Koen	103
QuesEr: Questions Eagerly Raised	Tawyeh Nishan-Do	105
Dead, Missing, or Alive?	Kimberly Cole	106
I Never Knew Lawrence	Michele Matthews	109
Foreign	Regina Jennings	111
Ice Cream vs. Stranger	Nkiru Nso-Ani	113

Contents

CHAPTER V
AMENDED: TIME AND FORGIVENESS HEALS ALL WOUNDS   116

Pimps Anonymous	Tina Fakhrid-Deen	118
To Err Is Human.	Jacqueline Olurin	121
To Forgive Divine		
Anthony Keith Reily	LaShaun Moore	123
Father Found	Jacquelin McCord	126
He Was Always There	Nadine McIlwain	129
Dust from the Past: Let it Settle	Joann Potts	133
Our Father Who Art in Heaven	Jacqueline Ward	135
Daddy	Charlene Hill	139
28 Years Later	Melda Beaty	141

CHAPTER VI
DECEASED: GONE TOO SOON   144

Moving On	Laylah Amatullah Barrayn	146
Selected Journal Entries	Jacinta V. White	150
of Jacinta V. White		
I Never Got to Know Him	Liberty R.O. Daniels	153
One Last I Love You	Ieesha Hearne	159
Never Too Late	Weena Stokes	162
He Wasn't a Myth; He Was a Man:	Vicki Meek	166
A Daughter's Revelation		
Premonition	Gloria Burgess	179
That Autumn Morning		180
My Father My Child	Louise E. Mitchell	181
Because You Loved Me...	Crystal Renae Braboy	184
Father's Day	Jennifer Margaret Wilks	186
Cancer Dad	Kimberly Rose	188

The Daughters: Contributor's Notes	193

Acknowledgements

To God be the glory! For it was Him who planted the seed in my head for a book about girls and their daddies when I was only 16-years-old, and who nurtured the seed/idea for 18 more years until the day it became a published copy. I have many "God incarnates" to thank for their unconditional support, patience, and labor in making this book a reality; to my mother, JoAnn Potts, who made me read a novel every summer from the age of eight and write her a book report, and who sparked my "vocabulary curiosity" by taking the time to engage me with numerous games of Scrabble. Warmest thanks to my husband, Peter Beaty, who built my first computer, which made it easier for me to record my 2 a.m. ideas, and for your selfless support of my desire to pursue my writing career while raising our daughter.

Thanks to Tony Armstrong for a website design that not only expresses the spirit of this book, but also expresses me. Thanks to my Editor, Teresa Fowler, for always being my second pair of eyes and a friend, and to Tiffany Pendleton for your maturity and ingenious typesetting.

I am blessed to have befriended some gracious women and men, who freely volunteered their time and talents to my vision: Lynnette Galloway (for your thoughtfulness—your creativity is pure genius), Stacy Klein (for answering every question and helping me stuff letters over hot chocolate), Jeannine Holmes (for your design ideas and your listserv connections), Taressa Stovall (for always giving it to me "straight with no chaser"), Dr. Trevy McDonald (for responding to my numerous emails with one publishing question after another), Pat Arnold (for your willingness to share information and realizing that we are in this publishing game together), Latonya Washington (for your legal wisdom and constant encouragement), Reverend Pamela Fox (for your spiritual guidance), Dr. Raquel Farmer-Hinton (for being my accountability partner and lifelong friend), and Charles Watkins (for always being a fan).

ACKNOWLEDGEMENTS

Lastly, there are people in your life whom you connect on a level that is spiritual in nature. Their presence in my life is necessary and their love is sustaining: Lawanda Ward and Angela McGee. I thank you both for being my lifelong kindred spirits.

And to the rest of my family, friends, and each contributor, this book exists because of you.

Introduction: AN EPIPHANY

I distinctly remember the only two times my father ever told me that he loved me. The first time was on Christmas Day 1984. I was 13 and upset that my father did not buy my brother and me any presents. I greeted Christmas morning with lips poked out and arms crossed. My mother relayed to my father that I was upset and made him explain the situation to his children. We sat on the edge of my parent's bed with my father sandwiched between us. He humbly explained that money was tight because he and my mother had just bought our home that summer, but he promised that he would get us something later. He concluded the scene with "I love you-all." I believed him.

The second and final time was ten years later. I was in graduate school and tired of making the bare minimum payments on a credit card that I foolishly acquired in college. I was saving for a car and wanted to eliminate all unnecessary debt. The last time I relied on my father for money was when he promised to pay my college tuition if I sent him the bill instead of to my mother. After sending him the statements every semester for a year, with a card or a letter enclosed, he chose not to respond to any of my correspondence or pay the tuition. My mother quickly became my financial rescue in times of need. I vowed never again to ask my father for one dime.

However, this time I was desperate and ready to give my father another chance. After all, I could count the number of times, on one hand, that I had asked my father for money since I had become an adult. After staring at his phone number all day and taking several deep breaths, I finally mustered the courage to dial the number. As the phone rang, my pride fought to renegotiate my needs.

At first my father was not entirely sure who had called so I tried to make small talk to give him time to recollect. I explained to him that I needed a car and was ready to buy one the first of the new year, but I still owed money (less than $400) on a credit card. I politely asked him if he could assist me with the final payment. He responded that he would and at that moment I felt a wave of embarrassment for being so afraid to call. I thanked him and before I hung up I said "love you daddy." He responded "love you too." He never sent the money and he never called. That is when the nightmares began.

For years after that conversation and the disappointment that followed, I had recurring nightmares about my father. They were always the same. In each one, my father and I would be in a crowded room and as soon as the crowd dispersed, as if on cue, I would immediately start shouting at him about how he had hurt me with all of his empty promises and his emotional neglect. I would yell, curse, cry and sometimes point my finger directly in his face. I would be so drained from the nightmares the next morning that I would lie in bed, fighting back the tears, while staring at the ceiling.

The nightmares hid me from the realities of pain and distrust. In them, I became a woman with a legitimate voice and feelings instead of a little girl steeped in fear in the presence of her daddy. In the nightmares, the anvil of hurt that weighed so heavily on my heart was replaced with bold and brazen strength, even if only in my dreams.

The reality between my father and I went far beyond missed Christmas presents, tuition payments, or credit card balances. Those incidents were merely superficial band-aids that covered years of emotional neglect.

Before I reached adolescence, our time together consisted of family vacations, walks to summer camp, and dinners together as a family. Gradually our home transformed into separate individuals living under the same roof passing each other in silence. I was a black teenage girl struggling to understand her development and identity while looking for the answers in friends and ultimately boys. I yearned for guidance, affirmation, and the type of love that reminds a young girl of her worth, beauty, and unlimited potential that only a father can give. I'm talking about a male love that is disconnected from possession, obsession, or penetration. There was never nor has there ever been an apology from my father, but more importantly there was never any forgiveness from me. Once I made up my mind to truly forgive him, the nightmares stopped.

For years after the nightmares, I thought I was the only one with a need to understand my relationship with my father. However, I have been blessed to meet, bond, and love other black women with similar and different childhood histories and complex father-daughter relationships. In our conversations, I noticed we questioned the same issues, reflected on similar experiences, engaged in unfulfilling relationships, and mutually understood life sometimes without even saying a word. We are living the effects of a loving or distant or non-existent relationship with our fathers. The effect of a father-daughter relationship for black women defines how we view and often how we engage in love with our husbands, boyfriends, sons, brothers, and friends.

My connection with these women and my own journey of self-exploration gave birth to the idea of a "safe space" for other sisters to share their sentiments toward their fathers in a candid and creative way. *My Soul to His Spirit: Soulful Expressions from Black Daughters to Their Fathers* is that safe space that examines that part of us that comes from our fathers and shapes the women we have become.

There are numerous books today that explore the relationships between fathers and daughters. A simple search on Amazon.com yields over 1,000 results; however, there is only one book that focuses exclusively on black women and their fathers, and the impact of "fatherlessness" for black women. Where is the voice of the black daughter? Black women are synonymous with nurturing, raising, and loving our families. It is a charge that was oftentimes forced on us from days of slavery when our black men were forcibly torn away from their families. Today, black women want to know "who will nurture, raise, and love us?" as we embark on this quest for fulfillment.

My Soul to His Spirit speaks to the totality of our lives as black women and the full spectrum of relationships with our fathers. All 63 authentic voices in this compilation, ranging in ages from 19-69, offer praise and even admiration for their fathers, as well as anger, confusion, forgiveness, and healing that often lies dormant in black women from childhood to adulthood.

While preparing for this book, I quickly realized that the experiences of my circle of friends were too small to represent the depth and breadth of father-daughter relationships. Surely every sister had a story to tell, so I set out to collect their stories. I sought the expressions from black women toward their fathers in the categories of **Loving, Distant, Abandoned, Non-Existent, Amended,** and **Deceased.**

My initial thoughts about a book that explored black father-daughter relationships were sparked by my college friends who simply adored their fathers. My collegiate peers were living proof that tangible, supportive, and loving relationships between girls and their daddies did exist. I wondered how many more of these relationships were there for other black women. I received the most submissions for loving father-daughter relationships than I could include in this compilation. Sisters were praising fathers who cooked breakfast in the morning, combed their hair, and called them on the phone just when they needed to hear a familiar voice. I begin *My Soul to His Sprit* with tributes to these loving fathers.

Following the section on "Loving" relationships is "Distant" relationships. I began to wonder; can a father love his daughter but at the same time keep his distance? Many of the stories describe relationships that are estranged by incidents like divorce or incarceration; however, the daughter is seeking to understand the role love plays during the separation.

When a distant relationship is distant for too long a young girl feels abandoned. All of a sudden there are no more visits, phone calls, or cards. What were once feelings of love and longing change to feelings of confusion and anger. In "Abandoned," their bold and fiery expressions begin to look inward for causes for his sudden disappearance.

Some fathers abandoned their daughters long before they ever had a chance to meet. I call this section "Non-Existent." Some of the writings in this section convey a stage in a black woman's life when she no longer cares to know her father's identity.

Other submissions recall stories they have heard about their fathers from relatives, or describe moments when they thought they recognized him in a crowd of strangers. The writings speak more to a daughter's resolution to accept his absence.

Whether he kept his distance, left in a hurry, or never made his presence known, many black women have or are ready to forgive. "Amended" father-daughter relationships are the "balms in Gilead." All of these women share their cathartic epiphanies with some fathers who womanized, severely disciplined, or forgot they existed. Their stories touch golden-rule principles that have universal appeal.

Lastly, "Deceased" showcases the sentiments for fathers who are no longer with us. Some of these fathers were loving, or distant, or abandoned, or non-existent. The point is that they are remembered by daughters who needed to express in words now what their heart could not during his life. Regardless of the category, I gave each woman the freedom to choose a written form of expression that best conveyed her innermost feelings. All I required were that the stories be true.

The women in this collection are wives, girlfriends, mothers, sisters, aunts, cousins, nieces, doctors, lawyers, teachers, students, administrators, executives, writers (published and non-published), and so much more. However, the commonality is that we all are daughters. Regardless of our status in life, we each have a story about our father that is expressed in the way that we learn, work, play, fight, dance, cry, laugh, live, and ultimately love.

Books have been written on the various factors that shape black women's lives, from our health to instructions on how to love and be loved. *My Soul to His Spirit* is one of the first books to explore the personal relationships that black daughters have with their fathers from the daughter's point of view. Writing for these women has become that emotional release. This labor of love has emerged to not only help black women understand the nature of relationships they have with their fathers and all men (husbands, sons, brothers, lovers, and friends), but to enlighten men on the impact they have on their daughter's lives.

In this compilation, you will meet and share in the lives of sisters whose fathers were once integral parts of their lives, but one day packed up their hearts and promises and abandoned their daughters in their formative years, adolescence, and adulthood. They left them when they needed them most with no forwarding address or date of their return.

Then there are sisters whose fathers eagerly and enthusiastically loved and supported their daughters. They attended their graduations, sporting events, interrogated their dates, encouraged their best, and walked them proudly down the aisle. These fathers continue to shower their daughters with unconditional love.

Some fathers choose to keep their distance. They make an appearance in their daughter's lives as it suits their schedules or needs. They may send a birthday card, a check, or call when they have heard through the grapevine that she has asked about them. These "every once in awhile" fathers make sporadic visits in their daughter's lives.

I cannot forget the sisters whose fathers were never there. There was no father to greet them when they emerged from their nine-month cocoon. There was no father to steady their tricycle as they learned to ride. There was no father to protect and warn them when their bodies started commanding the attention of onlookers. His whereabouts remain a mystery. If they were to meet, would they recognize each other or would they simply pass each other on the street? His absence has been replaced with anger, confusion, and pain.

What about those sisters who had to bury a father whose love enriched their lives. Some of those fathers had the privilege of knowing their daughters before death came calling, while others did not. These daughters of the deceased share their sentiments of a father gone too soon.

INTRODUCTION

Now there is this new breed of women whose life is purged in catharsis. They have harbored a plethora of emotions toward their fathers for almost the whole of their lives. Somewhere along the way their fathers violated their trust, failed their expectations, and avoided his responsibilities. Instead of choosing defeat, these women are waving their white flags and announcing to the world, "time and forgiveness heals all wounds."

I am one of these daughters and I humbly accept my role as midwife. I, along with the women in this collection, made a conscious choice to know more about ourselves through our relationships with our fathers.

As these daughters reveal their souls to the living or deceased spirits of their fathers, read them with more than your minds. Allow your hearts to embrace the experience so that the strengthening and healing of the black family may begin and/or continue, and we are all one step closer to completion.

~Melda Beaty

Loving
DADDY'S GIRL

"You are the standard to
which I hold all men."

"I am resilient because he is. I am strong
because he is. I am proud because he is."

"... for all his goodness has
left me blind at times."

CHAPTER I

Loving: DADDY'S GIRL

*D*espite statistics, stigmas, and the 5:00 nightly news, there are and have been black men who are mainstays in their daughter's lives. He is the first one whom she credits for emotional, financial, and often spiritual support in her life because he was there. According to Reverend Pamela Fox, LCSW/M.Div, Foxfire Outreach Ministries in Chicago, Illinois, a loving father is the "rites of passage" in a black woman's life. These fathers are following the biblical blueprint of what it means to be a caring father. The Bible asks the question of all fathers, "Which of you, if his son {daughter} asks for bread, will give him a stone? Or if he asks for a fish, will give him a snake?" Bread and fish are synonymous with the good and necessary parts of life that a girl needs. His unconditional presence in her life is her bread and her fish.

The loved daughters in this opening chapter willingly classify themselves as "daddy's girls." Their stories of homage to these men overflowed my mailbox with tender words that poetically and melodiously narrate a father-figure that every girl, if only while reading these stories, can love. A black woman who is nurtured by her father accepts nothing less in her mate, values sacrifice, and insists that future generations of black men carried in her womb appreciate and understand the importance of family.

These "daddy's girls" invite you to share in the love they have for their fathers and witness the impact his love has on her life.

A Loving Dad

- Adina Jordan Andrews

*D*addy, I don't see it. They say we're most alike. I carry no special place-ment in the birth order. I am not your eldest, nor your son. We both pinch pennies and plan. We must be on time. You are 30 years my senior almost to the day. Your intellectual passions are always more spontane-ous and disciplined. Verbal musings roll from your tongue as a splendid waterfall. My expressions take greater deliberation. As a child, I thought you were brilliant and wondered at the ideas that sprang from you. When we listened—when you made us listen during dinner, I was embarrassed when friends happened by, and you invited them in. They were uncom-fortable. So was I, because they were there. My favorite playmates were intruders to our circle of rapt, like my squirming sisters, and baby brother engaging in our daily occasion of hearing your words sifting on and around us. Your eloquent thundering to their simplest questions was foreign to the monosyllabic adult responses to which my playmates were accus-tomed. They didn't know the world was your stage. When you released us from the table, I thought to apologize for our family's "discussion," but joined in the hot fray of dodge ball outside.

***

I never knew a father and mother could not be together until Moth-er told me my best friend Wanda's parents down the street were getting divorced. "Divorced?" A word I was big enough to know. Attempting to understand Wanda living with only her mother, while her father was still alive was a repellant imagination. To grasp Wanda's plight, I visually re-created myself without you. My six-year-old life saw horrific emptiness. My mind would not hold it. Neither Riverview, nor grandmother Julia's laugh could fill it. Going to Riverview with only my sisters and my brother and my mother? I saw no joy in it. My imaginings painted you back in.

***

We laughed and laughed when we girls climbed to the upstairs back window to wait. From Calumet to Michigan Avenue, we could see a bus slow to a stop. You stepped down in front of the evening sun and walked past our open play fields upon which builders were clamoring to place new brick boxes. "Daddy!" We laughed and laughed. From five blocks away, we decided the color of your shirt, as it bobbed in the warm air, was an umbrella. Resting on our knees, foreheads pushing the window screen, the umbrella transformed before our scientific gaze into your tall graceful stride. So as not to be accused of fabrication, we went to our summer evening window day after day to watch the umbrella turn into Daddy every time. What a clamor. Your welcome home from your umbrella walk. Daddy's home. "Daddy! Daddy!" Mother was first. You took too long. Kissing her in front of us. Too long. We were next. Skinny arms, one by one, reaching to the ceiling where we found you.

***

"Ooooh, how keee-ute!" Another nosy lady on her way to church. Around her neck a brown animal, dead, with five small heads staring, teeth and all, and claws that dangled and swayed when the bus stopped. "Are these your girrrrls?" Who else's? I thought. The whole world on the bus turned to look. Elegantly, you answered her. "Ohhhh. Going to Sunday school," she said. "How sooweeet." Of course that's where we're going. You were the superintendent of Sunday school! "This is the big girl," you explained exquisitely to her and the bus world...."The middle girl and the baby girl." "Oh, oh, oh," she cooed, clasping her gloved hands. "Those pretty little dresses. And who fixed their hair?" I was getting carsick on the bus and turned to count the whizzing street signs outside.

***

Out of control. Mother said I was, years later. I assume she referred to my experiment. I was getting hard to handle. Ranting, raving. The usual, to see how far I could go, without incurring a life sentence. You and mother met secretly and decided you needed to change your work hours back from nights to days to be at home during my experiments in terror. Mother said it was the Wanda influence. She said I was back to normal when you were home for dinners.

***

I didn't know what to do with my arms. My legs too. Was I tall? Short? Mother still braided my hair. Two were enough. One. Two. One in the front. One in the back. No fancy hair do, thank you. Growing up was OK, but running forever in humid summers was better. What to do with my arms? I saw Kevin from around the corner swinging his and hunch his shoulders. I decided to copy him for a few days. You spoke to me quietly, very quietly, like I was an adult, and told me to walk nicely, like a young lady.

***

Boring. Summer was boring. Mother made me go all the way downtown to learn to play golf, and Ping-Pong. I know how to play volleyball, and they tried to teach me that, too! Catastrophe! The only black girl! The place not even air-conditioned. What a joke! Hot and boring like everything else!

Mother still greets you with a kiss when you come home to dinner. So does everyone else—but me. Big deal. Life changes, you know. What's the big fat deal? You noticed my distance. You told me so. The gentle pain in your throat was there.

***

My trunk was packed for days. Was this a rite of passage? A test of nerves? Leaving home for school, I mean college, wasn't at all exciting. It was nerve wrecking. Well, I made my choice. After pouring weeks and weeks over the College Board manual, I selected the most exotic, cost-effective state school in Illinois. You told us we could not leave the state, nor go to a private college. Too expensive. No debt, no debt was your edict! So, after feeling my way around the country college town, and making friends with mostly black students, who called me 'sistah,' I decided I was not home sick. The many family dinner discussions we had over issues affecting our community honed my radar as I began articulating ideas and concepts special to our People. I was using your ideas as my own. I referenced you often. If a twinge of homesickness set in, I called collect, frequently. Mother's melodic voice, and your rich tones, helped. One day you said softly that you loved me very much, and to begin writing home instead. Oh! That's reasonable!

***

I wept. I was completing my undergraduate years, and I was broken. I sobbed and sobbed in the phone, no longer the cool pillar, the much quieter female shadow of you. When mother answered, I asked for you and cried so. Devastating pain that could wreck the strongest. The effects of first love gone completely haywire. You listened. And listened. From long distance you listened.

***

"Spending Thanksgiving with your Mother?" She was the third person to ask. "With my parents," I corrected. When did I begin noticing their exclusion of you? That it made me wince? Your insignificance is profiled in subtle ways. I'm sure you've always known this. They never saw you on stage; acting in community theatres, or celebrated when you completed your college degree with four children coming out of the woodwork. They didn't consider you were always with us. Always. How many sons

~12~

and daughters have you "adopted" —our friends and others who sought your ear and counsel on personal, social and political matters? Your quiet humility belies this. Remember when Mother was the first of her friends to sport an Afro? It was your idea, and you cut her hair.

Long ago, us girls decided "Mommy" was not in keeping with our new sophistication. "Mother" clumsily rolled out of our mouths, for a while, until it became as endearing as the woman she is. We postponed your renaming. I watch you stride with your African walking stick supporting you. Supporting your growing age. You're 80, and your middle daughter still calls you Daddy.

"Growing old is fascinating!"
you announce.

Staying Afloat: Because of Him

- Michelle D. Parrish

I am my mother's daughter, but I am my father's child. People who have never met me know that I am his. I look like him. I talk like him. I think like him. We don't always agree. We argue with the same passion...with the same concern...with the same fears. No means no with us. We speak our own language. We drink coffee and talk about music. I sometimes want to protect him like he is my brother. For the cause, we stand up together, we lay down together, we die together—whatever that cause may be.

He used to open my mail and read my financial statements. He never opened the letters from jail. He just shook his head as if possibly he were seeing himself in me. I am the breath of his spirit. I am the son he always wanted. I am the daughter that he has needed.

Reading picked-over, open bank statements; I was red with fury... with anger...with rage. I lashed out at him. I yelled at him. I told him that I hated him. I started sending my mail to my best friend's house, but certain things cannot be hidden. So I gave in. I bit the bullet. I saved. I bought a car. I moved out. I damn near drowned.

I cried a lot. I never told him. I pretended to have strength—to be able to stay afloat—to be able to climb my way to the top. I found a way out. He did not agree. He did not understand why I did it: why I had moved to the suburbs and chosen a roommate. I survived. I became strong. I lived through it.

I am resilient because he is. I am strong because he is. I am proud because he is. I hide my fears because he does. Neither of us is as strong a swimmer as my mother, but we refuse to drown. She is our lifeguard... the softer side of us. I love my father to an extent that cannot be measured in any words.

Papi Was a Dancing Man

(dedicated to Zenithia & Kito)

- Avotcja

Papi was 25 shades blacker than midnight
Blue-Black, they called him
         Papi
    was a "Pretty-boy"
Skin so smooth .....
He looked like he was carved out of ebony
Papi never just walked
He was smooth like his skin,
     moved like a panther,
        like a well sung song
Papi was beautiful to watch,
     wore his pride like armour,
        like a weapon,
           like a shield
In cities designed to make him disappear
He wore his blackness like a badge of honor
     moved through the whiter than thou madness
        with the grace of greased lightening
Danced his way across stages
     that tried to bury him
        in the filth of "their" fear
Papi was 25 shades blacker than midnight
The kind of unstoppable Black
     that "they" couldn't hold back
        no matter how much "they" tried
Papi was untouchable
Even when "they" tried to get at him
     by trying to get to me
He danced in "their" faces
     on all "their" sacred places
        and made a joke of "their" ignorance

By stealing "their" shows (on "their" stages), and
      giving unasked for lessons on the real Black Power
          his unshakeable power
              our undeniable survival power
        Papi
Papi was 25 shades blacker than midnight
25 times blacker than was tolerable
      by terrified white folks
          by immaculate "knee-grow" jet setters

Hair "too bad" to be so confident
      too African looking to be so proud
        Toooo LOUD to be so arrogant
          Too damn Black (or so "they" said)
But, even when Black was
      a never to be spoken word
          "they" couldn't stop his beauty
I mean, like
      when Papi smiled
          even the wind held its breath
And while all the foolish tongues rattled ... he danced
He danced, and spread his Blackness .....
      across the whiteness of this stolen land
And he danced, and danced, and danced, and danced,
      and kept holding my hand
Held on real tight 'til I was strong enough .....
      to see the light & write this poem
Papi was 25 shades blacker than midnight

Loving Daddy

- Suzetta M. Perkins

Number one girl," my daddy yells as he calls out in rapid succession, the names of his eight children until he finds mine and announces his discovery. I revel in that sound, often imitating my father's cadence in my attempt to recall the names of my own two children.

In the beginning and now, 52 years later, I've had the distinct pleasure of knowing that I was loved. In the countless photographs my daddy took of my brother and me, posed one way or another to capture the essence of who we were, you could see the love that exuded from the pages of those timeless gems. And to have the exclusive honor of being my father's first born or number-one girl, which he affectionately calls me to this day, does have its advantages.

Growing up in the 50s and in Oakland, California was a remarkable time to live. There were many opportunities for us there, and my daddy who was the lone bread winner saw to it that his family had want for nothing, and reaped the benefits that our life in a not-so-harsh environment afforded. This was the era when families were wholesome, vibrant, and believed a family that "prays together stays together." My parents were of the mindset that if that is what daddy or momma said then that was the conclusion of the matter. They were one—a formidable team united on all fronts.

My business sense, taste in clothes, love for the arts, and frequent flyer travel is another act of the dominant Y-chromosome given to me at birth. Three-piece-suits, color-coded underwear, long and short-sleeved shirts, and gorgeous ties that would make an artist mad were my father's trademark—and he groomed his daughter well.

Reciting James Weldon Johnson's *The Creation* was once a frightening experience for me after being asked to perform it in front of an audience and then compared to my father's delivery of the same infamous poem. I am a reflection of my daddy, and while we have never admitted this out loud, the uncanny parallel is hard to miss.

I don't believe I was a bonafide daddy's girl. Our similar thinking patterns and sense of creativity bonded us close together. Our desire to excel in whatever we put our minds to do, whether it was to become a writer or become the best real estate broker, was always our goal, and we would often consult each other to explore and examine the other's thoughts on the matter. Daddy was special, and I was an extension of him.

There were moments when I believed love didn't have a face. Those awkward teenage years when hormones take flight and you discover yourself, things about yourself that deserve further examination were the most difficult times in my relationship with my father. I wanted to explore and feel free to do what most teenagers my age were able to do without having to validate every action I wanted to take. However, my hands and feet were tied, because my daddy had laid down a thick set of rules to save me from myself, and, of course, preserve our family's good name. I needed a passport just to get out the door if I wanted to go somewhere other than school, choir rehearsal, and church.

And while father and daughter were at odds on many issues during those formidable years, I came to realize as my parents had so often claimed, they knew what was good for me and that someday when I grew up, got married, and had children of my own, I would understand the full scope of what they had made a conscious effort to impress upon me most of my life.

Tuesday, September 11, 2001, held as much meaning to me as those who mourned the tragic deaths of their loved ones—victims of terrorism. It was also the last time I spoke with my mother. She had a heart attack 19 days later. My mother and father were best friends and celebrated 50 years of wedded bliss only a few months earlier. My father lost his oyster, his pearl, his world, and is today still overcome at the loss of my mother.

I have truly become daddy's girl, daddy's number-one girl. Sometimes I wish I could rub his back until the pain goes away...and it will eventually. I wish I could bring my mother back so my daddy won't be lonely...so I won't be lonely—so I can see my daddy's smile once again that lights up the midnight sky whenever my mother is near.

As always, daddy's girl is there when daddy wants to recount that tragic day for the fifteenth time. Daddy's girl is there to offer prayer to help lift the spirit of his fragile and broken heart. Daddy's girl gives wise counsel to help daddy on the road to recovery. And daddy leans on number-one girl's shoulder as he soaks up her love and feels his belly to capacity, hoping it will sustain him until the next time his number-one girl calls—and I am hoping it will sustain me until the next time I speak with my daddy.

Daddy's Eyes

- Tauheedah Shakoor-Strong

Your eyes said you are my pride
Black like me don't run don't hide
Precious pearl go brighten the world
The gifts inside will unfurl

911, oh dad can't you see
Need your eyes right here with me
In my little-girl purse clutched at my side
So I can reach in pull out my pride

Wanted to turn to stop the chase
To flash their glow to end the haste
No need for ridicule no lashes for me
Beautiful in black as meant to be

Instead I ran waited by the door
For daddy's eyes to mend me once more

You entered with eyes of a romantic composer
Watched you wrap my mother in pink roses
A portrait of hearts in sweet assurance
A love to last guaranteed endurance

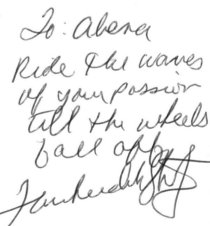

To: Abena
Ride the waves
of your passion
till the wheels
fall off
Tauheedah

You set the mark then and there
To share my soul requires a fare
No fly by night no time-share
Only pure love from the wings of a prayer

You worked extra hours long and hard
Filled our holidays, no holds barred
Loved the way you dressed to the nine
The twinkle in your eyes at Christmas time
The tree wasn't quite right it appeared
Til stumbling in delight you christened it with cheer

MY SOUL TO HIS SPIRIT

And then there were the battle-burned eyes
Witnessed your clinging, the chase, your cries
No doubt wartime left you with scars
Second-class citizen stripped and marred
You said I fought to come home you see
I am no killer still they made one of me

Left the South for a better life indeed
To give my family the good I perceived
Can't help with homework or plan your career
I've little education I'm sorry my dear
Looked into the eyes that hid
The guilt the shame of a robbed kid

Struggled to hold back tear-filled eyes
Would not pity the man of my pride
Wanted to say something to you
Knew your pain but not what to do

I tended the veggies and picked the fruits
A city girl grew southern roots
We drew clear water from the spring you found
Fresh air, open country makes me cry out loud
I gained strength from the labor you knew
And hoped in time you saw I loved you

Rise you did fire in your eyes
Determined to face-off no run no hide
Stood at your side in case you needed me
Rejoiced as you grew tall as an oak tree
You stepped in honoring yourself
I learned to be free above all else

You and I so much alike
Quiet and shy yet full of life
Eyes that speak what words cannot
Project our passion spell our thoughts

Held your hand your eyes at rest
Shallow breath hollow chest
Even in the moment of release

You still impart insight to me
That Spirit is breath and breath carries life
Riding the waves I'll reach my height
Nestled in its peace I find
A powerful Light that shines through all time

Close out the outer then I see
Sparkling eyes inside of me
You in me I with thee
Forever loved forever free

Daddy's Little Girl

- Gabriella Miller

I remember the day in 1976 when you held me up to look into Mommy's casket. She was wearing a pink dress with white lace. Her expression was peaceful as if she was in a deep, restful sleep. It is as if that 26-year-old image was planted in my head yesterday. I truly thought that she was sleeping. You knew that I did not understand. The feelings of anguish, fear, and uncertainty must have been dizzying as you absorbed your new reality: losing your love and raising a three-year-old daughter, alone, in the rural back roads of eastern North Carolina. Sometime after the funeral, I remember putting my hands around your neck telling you that everything was going to be okay. Although innocent and naïve, I was right.

All things work together for the good of them who love the Lord
and who are called according to His purpose.
-Romans 8: 28

I can't say that everyday was easy, but with you, Daddy, I never wanted for anything—your time, your affection, your energy, and your persistent discipline. Through the eyes of a 29-year-old mother, I can comprehend the magnitude of the sacrifices that you made for me. Remember when we first moved from North Carolina to Des Plaines, Illinois? Money was extremely tight. We were on our way to visit Aunt Gladys in Chicago and you told me that you only had three dollars. I smile every time I think of this. You told the kid with the biggest mouth on earth, not to tell anyone about our situation. In hindsight, I think you did that on purpose.

I did not tell Aunt Gladys, because I feared we'd go hungry. I told her because I was glad to have some grown-up conversation. Oh, the innocence of youth. You never gave me an opportunity to grow resentful, even though I found myself daily explaining why I didn't have a mother. You inundated me with the word of God through bible stories, church, CCD classes, and gospel music. Your submission and faithfulness to God, even though he took your precious Carol, led me to God. Daddy, because of your example, I have a heart for God. My unshakeable faith and submission to God is a testament to the fact that you—a 31-year-old man, in the prime of his life and career, left alone to raise a three-year-old daughter, did not turn from Him when no one would have blamed you for doing so. You were my father, my mother, my best friend, and for a long time you were my god—I adored you to the point of worship.

People were always amazed that you knew how to cook and comb my hair. You pressed my hair, you curled my hair, and you dressed me well. Sometimes I was amazed at the things you learned to do. I often wonder what our lives would have been like if Mommy had lived, but as strange as it sounds, I love the life that we had because I was your little girl.

When I grow up, I want to marry a man just like my Daddy.

I remember the day that Aamon asked you for my hand in marriage. You and Ma were sitting on one side of the dining room table, Aamon and I sitting on the other side. You listened patiently, nodded your approval to Aamon and then began to cry. At that moment, I believe you felt the exact way I felt in 1982 when you told me that you were getting married—elation, approval, anticipation all mixed with sadness, maybe even a tinge of jealousy.

My nod of approval in 1982 signaled the end of our relationship, as I had known it—me as the center of your world. Your nod of approval on that November day in 1994 signaled the end of our relationship, as you had known it—you as the center of my world.

Daddy it is because of your love, your example, your relationship with God, your relationship with my new mother, that I can give the testimony that, "All things work together for the good of them that love the Lord and are called according to His purpose." I love you, Daddy and, in my heart, I am still your little girl.

The Essence of Manhood

- Tedella Gowans

The mystery of the black man was unlocked when I was a baby gazing into my dad's eyes. I knew he looked different than my mom, more cinnamon/caramel than mahogany. I knew he had a banana nose that I would grab, just because it was there.

As a young child, I remember my dad would pick out my clothes and do my hair (not just one braid either). He was very meticulous, so the parts had to be perfectly straight. He made sure that the hair ornaments matched whatever I was wearing. Most Saturday mornings, since we only had one bathroom, I would sit on the toilet lid and watch him shave or brush his teeth. Sometimes I would brush my teeth with him and remind him not to spit on the back of my head. We would talk and laugh to the point where my mom would tell us to "shut up." We would stop talking for a moment, and then I would look up at him and say, "Guess she told you." He would cut his eye at me and I would start laughing and grabbing my belly.

I remember when I discovered my dad was the smartest man on the planet. We were sitting in his van waiting for it to warm up, and I asked him why smoke came out of my mouth (I really did not think he would have an answer). He told me that because my body temperature was higher than the outside temperature, when the two opposite air masses collide a condensation is formed...I was amazed and impressed.

There were many opportunities when my dad impressed me: he could make a whistle by putting his two hands together, he could make teacups and saucers, Jacobs ladder, the spider, and with just a piece of string, he could turn a simple cardboard box into a working castle. He could also make the meanest breakfast (French toast, garlic cheese eggs, and sausage... mmm).

When I became a woman, I knew my dad loved me, but I did not hear him say it that often. One day, when I was away at college, I spoke with he and my mom and he knew that I was struggling in one of my subjects. After we had the conversation and I was about to say goodbye, he said "I love you kid" (of course I was stunned and later called my mother to see if he was OK). I guess it was on that day that he felt comfortable to share his feelings with me, though limited.

Now that I am living on my own, and have had encounters with other women's sons, I can indeed say that my father is the mold upon which others should be formed. I do not truly know the 'man' of my dad, but what has been revealed to me has set the standard for the comparison for my future husband. I know based on my dad that he has to be his own man, know what he wants, motivated to take care of his family, have his own interest, but at least be willing to share in mine, supportive, knowledgeable, and most of all have his own "love language."

My dad, with all his faults, is the quintessential man.

The First Man to Love Me:

James Bernice Brown

- Angela D. Gittens

"Don't you hurt your daddy's feelings by telling him he can't come to your award ceremony at school."

"But Mama, it's embarrassing having him be the only father there. He doesn't have to take off work just for a simple ceremony. It's not really that important."

"Girl, he's proud of you. So you just let him be proud, and he'll be there for you."

Thank you for being there, daddy. Even when I had no idea how much balance it would add to my life, you knew. When I put on the little dresses with the patent leather shoes and frilly socks, you made me feel like the prettiest girl on earth. When I put on the long fitted dresses with sheer stockings and high heels, you told me I looked like a princess. Each time after you took out your wallet and showed off Mama's picture while calling her your "big baby," you flipped to the next picture (of me) and showed them your "little baby."

When I stayed up alone at times working on school projects until 2:00 a.m. on weeknights, I discovered that I was not the only person awake after all. In silence, you waited up with me just to offer moral support, because you knew I was so overwhelmed with work, and not once did you complain of being tired from your own day's work. You only asked me if there was anything you could do to help. On evenings when you worked second shift at the hospital, I waited anxiously for you to come home, because you always made the house foundation feel complete. And how I loved watching you love Mama. We saw only huge cards and big kisses, wide smiles and utter bliss in your eyes for "the love of your life." If Sarah and I could get a man like you, we knew we would be blessed with nothing but the best.

When you took me away to college, your flowing tears started a river that made it hard for us to part. You were never too strong or too proud to show your love, and my heart would always melt at the mere sight of your love in action. What a great job you have done holding your family together. The boys always had your support and your presence through each stage of their lives. In spirit, mind, and body, your strength stood out heads above the rest as other families in our church even voted you "Man of the Year." And Mama was head over heels in love with you, her man. The pleasurable moments stand out in my mind, but the hard times are also crystal clear.

When you were diagnosed with Parkinson's disease, you were disappointed only to know that there might come a day when you would not be able to continue to support your family. So you kept on working. You stood at work in the operating rooms until you were too weak to stand for so long and your hands started to shake, so you retired before your due time. You drove and walked to church until your motor skills no longer allowed you to drive and you began to use a wheelchair. Your children pushed you around in the chair until you became bedridden, and even during Mama's illness, she kept you exercising so that you wouldn't feel "no ways tired." And when we had to lift you from the bed to help you stretch your limbs, I understood your sadness. You didn't have to speak; I understood your non-verbal language. I, your baby daughter, understood that you only wanted to continue being the strong husband, father, brother, and uncle that you were.

I knew when it was time for you to cross the river to the "other side," for I saw it in your eyes. Without Mama, and without your independence, I knew you were ready to go.

Thank you, daddy. For being the first man to show me what real love is all about; for showing me strength in humility; for walking the walk and not just talking the talk; for helping a little girl, a developing teenager, and a young lady to see the essence of her natural beauty through your eyes. You were a father not only to the five of us, but to hundreds of others. Thank you for being there and for attending those award ceremonies after all. Being blessed to have had a father such as you, it is I who am the proud one.

Lessons from My Father

- Pamela Gilmore

As a child, I remember looking up at the giant towering above me. With large brown hands, he leaned down and swept me up and held me in powerful arms. I knew I was safe from harm. Throughout my life I have felt that safety—the quiet reassurance that no matter what happens, those large brown hands would protect me. It is with this feeling that I tackled life, each endeavor, and each challenge. With time, I am able to reminisce about talks around the kitchen of psychological profiles and personality development of the criminal mind. We both shared interest in Psychology—as he held a degree in Psychology and I pursued one.

All conversations were not about the state of the world, but instead concerned the state of me. Sometimes, I was wrestling with problems and sought answers as a teen growing into adulthood, or as an adult still learning about the world. With outstretched legs, he would lean back in his chair with quiet reserve posing more questions than he answered. I would expect words of wisdom to pour from his mouth revealing life's secret to happiness and fulfillment. Instead he would smile and with arms folded he would say in a low voice, "What do you think you should do?" This response always bewildered me, but I soon realized what he was trying to teach. It was his way of forcing me to find my way to the solution, rather than just giving me the answer. He was in his own way guiding me towards inner strength when I felt weak, while learning to listen to the inner voice inside of me. It took awhile for me to learn that as I fumbled from adolescence into early adulthood.

Still he was there watching me tread water, but never letting me drown. He stood quietly by as he watched me slowly grow with the inner strength he already possessed.

Those invisible large brown hands would scoop me up when it seemed I was going under, and I am grateful for that. He was a man who had to rely on that inner strength, the quiet reserve, and his intellect to be the man he had become. In 1967, it was that strength that allowed him to walk into riotous streets—when it was killing season against cops. He went to work each day as his fellow officers were killed hoping he would not be next.

He was barely out of the police academy when his indoctrination into the police force was riot control. It was the beginning of years of violence towards blacks and particularly towards black cops. At the time both the Black Panthers and the Black Liberation Army were out to kill cops. Looking back, I can see that he never allowed his fears to show.

Witnessing him transition from a police officer to a funeral director, I have learned to make the most of my skills while being the best I can be. From him I have been shown perseverance and determination, while learning compassion. He never told me how to live life, but showed me how to make the best of whatever life put in my path and because of this I have been able to endure the "storms" and enjoy the "sun." As an adult, I now realize all he has tried to teach me—the life lessons he showed by example. I see now the gift he tried to give me was me.

My Husband Got a Job on His Hands

- Kotanya K. Kimbrough

My future husband got a job on his hands
Because in my life there has been another man
From the beginning of the beginning of my life you see
One of his roles in this life was to watch over me

He would often watch from the doorway of my room
I'd see his silhouette caused by the reflection of the moon
At my softball games, he would hide behind small trees
So he could show support and not be a distraction to me

His hands, so thick, big and strong
My hand like his, equally as long
I remember a thump in the middle of my head
I cried so hard you would have thought someone dead

"Pete and Repeat" is what they called no doubt
"He looked like he chewed you up and spit you out"
I always hated that saying, even to this day
But truly I wouldn't have it any other way

My husband got a job on his hands
Because in my life there has been another man
From the beginning of the beginning of my life you see
One of his roles in this life was to watch over me

He was the protector, provider, and priest in home
Was a preacher, teacher that taught us we were never alone
For if he was not with us, God surely was
Not because of our goodness, but because of his love

This man dipped me in pool as a symbol of God's grace

And then cleaned the water from my seven-year-old face
"Think, Think, Think," was often heard
Almost more than God's word

This man would read everything in sight
And ivory bones slamming' the table night after night
This man could make his food look so good
And when I ate off his plate he understood

Oh my future husband got a job on his hand
Because in my life there has been another man
I hope he understands if he doesn't that is too bad
Because that other man is my DAD.

Giant Revealed:
For Dad

- Sandra Morris

My earliest remembrance was looking up
Into a smiling face with kind, slanted eyes like mine.
Strong arms threw me up in the air
As I laughed towards the sun.

His delighted chuckles rumbled
As I snuggled closer for stories about his boy days.
There I would drink in that comforting scent,
Feeling cocooned in security.

Sometimes I would flip through his mountain of tomes
While he watched indulgently
And stoked the curiosity that bloomed within me
About the peculiar science of people.

Then I grew up.

This larger than life figure
Was just a man.
Who erred, who battled, who disappointed.
But this giant revealed
Is the one who taught me
To create,
Hold fast
And dare to live my dreams.

A Father's Lesson by Example

- Denise L. Johnson

When I became conscious, at about age five, it quickly became apparent in the 60s that black people worked all the time. Despite stereotypes on radio and television, all of my neighbors, uncles, and cousins worked two or more jobs daily and went to school.

Our parents were WWII survivors, benefactors of the GI Bill. Now our fathers, who would have not been able to afford a college education, could do so with support of the government. My dad, like so many others, worked in the post office, other low-level government jobs, drove a taxi at night, and went to school at Roosevelt College in the evenings. I did not think this was unusual, because almost all of our neighbors were involved in this round-the-clock work ethic.

Despite the hectic schedule, my dad took us to Lake Michigan on Sundays. The pure delight in his time with us at the beach is captured in a picture that I treasure. He is sitting in the wet sand with his children, and he is imitating us, as we put wet sand over our heads, hair, and face. My usual, stern dad looked like one of his children, unbridled joy and love.

My mother, a beautiful, strong, woman was quite a match for my dad. Both parents grew up in Vicksburg, MS. Dad was class president, valedictorian, and bandleader in high school. Mom was the proverbial bookworm, quiet, self-absorbed and also valedictorian in her year. My dad pursued her and convinced her to elope at the age of 17 instead of attending college on a full scholarship.

Her decision to not pursue a college education and graduate education often became a topic of repeated arguments over the years. However, dad would always say, that he wanted a smart woman in his life, even one who challenged him continually.

Dad was unconventional. For some reason, he talked to me, his eldest, all of the time. I mean all the time. During television shows, piano practice, and shopping. My dad believed in women's liberation before its time. I had the long hair of the 60s, straightened to death, flipped and utterly lifeless. Over my mother's protests, dad cut my hair and shaped it into a beautiful Afro...Go figure. My mother threatened to leave him over that one.

Lately, I have been haunted by one of the many adventures with my dad. I have often wondered why my dad took me to an area of Chicago known as "skid row" as a child. It was a melancholy period of my dad's life, I am sure. Of course, as a child, I didn't realize that, but I stayed with him, my Papa, through it all.

During one of our trips to skid row, he asked me to look into the eyes of some of the men who were in various stages of alcohol and substance abuse, in disarray, mentally disturbed, and a little smelly. As a young girl of maybe six or seven, this was not the outing one would consider a "great day" with dad. Instead of the usual popcorn or cotton candy, we shared a Chicago polish sausage.

However, something has always stuck with me from the conversations we would have as we walked the streets while the men asked for money. It must have looked odd for a nicely dressed black man and his little girl to walk through those desolate streets. My dad told me that many of those men were probably brilliant, but somehow may have lost their way, lost their will, and used other "things" to help them make it.

He also told me sometimes people just want to get lost, to get away from life. He taught me not to judge, pity, or have disdain for them, but to understand how it can happen to anyone of us. He somehow, imparted to my young mind, that life could challenge even the greatest intellect. That you cannot judge anyone based on his or her particular circumstances.

We sat in a half-way house one afternoon and talked to a toothless, old, white man who explained his leadership at one of Chicago's leading universities. A change in circumstances and increased alcohol dependence landed him homeless and without family support. That toothless old man was so touched by the fact that my dad and I took the time to listen.

Of all of the lessons my dad imparted, this lesson, and these experiences with the "skid row" white man, have haunted me. I wondered as I became older, if my dad ever wanted to run away, to become invisible in his own country in order to avoid the disappointments of everyday life, of racism, of failures, both real and imagined. That small insight into my dad, as a human being, has provided a foundation for me when I have felt overwhelmed.

Daddy's Hardworking Hands

- Virginia K. Lee

loved to caress daddy's hardworking hands
caddied golf, cut grass, waited dining cars
African-American father of eight loyal fans

poured steel, fixed autos, scrubbed pots/pans
pumped gas, mopped floors, opened jars
loved to caress daddy's hardworking hands

a kind-hearted deacon lived by God's commands
no hangouts, street corners, night clubs/bars
African-American father of eight loyal fans

bore burden of life's countless demands
never rude or crude, enjoyed King Edward cigars
loved to caress daddy's hardworking hands

strong as Samson's yet issued gentle reprimands
years of toil evidenced by calluses and scars
African-American father of eight loyal fans

liked driving long, shiny black sedans
handsome debonair looks rivaled movie stars
loved to caress daddy's hardworking hands
African-American father of eight loyal fans

Precious Lord

- Virginia K. Lee

was my dad's
favorite hymn

whenever I hear it
I see his broad smile
cigar clenched
between his teeth

the aroma wraps
around me
like his loving arms

I hear his long steps
on the pavement
and baritone words
calling me   Jen

the creases in his
khaki work pants
are crisp and straight

as he tinkers with
a broken toaster
or bends under
a car hood in the
California sun to

replace a spark plug
adjust a carburetor
black grease under
his fingernails

sweat on the band
of his straw hat
brown plaid handkerchief
wipes his suntanned brow

he is always working
always fixing
until the Lord takes his
hand and leads him on....

Surely He Knows This

- Julie Amari-Bandele

I remember. She laughed so hard, and I think her smile could light up the whole world. And I wonder if he knows it's simply because he came in the room. She loves my mother, yes—who else knows children better than my mother? But my father...he is like magic to her. Surely, he knows this. Funny, I never told him.

And even now, now that we live thousands of miles apart, nothing can end the fury of this two-year-old's tantrum like the mention of "Papa's truck." Surely he knows this. Funny, I never told him.

They say two year olds are fickle. That's why they clamor to talk on the phone and run away when you hand it to them. My daughter is THE master of this. No begging, cajoling or pleading can make her say anything into that mouthpiece. Nothing, except the words: "It's Papa!" Surely he knows this? Funny, I never told him.

It seems that everything about a two-year-old's world is about discovery. I can't help but smile when something my father tells her elicits that sacred: "Wow!" or a gleeful giggle. Though the magic of her relationship with him, my father again seems so magical to me. I realize how much I love my father. Surely he knows this? Funny, I never told him.

Dancing on Daddy's Feet

- Akua Lezli Hope

He was our brown Fred Astaire
thin, dashing, fleet-footed hero
time stepping, sand shuffling,
 tapping   twirling,
doing that click toe touch up our stairs

elegant line from head to finger
or shoulderwinged back architected moves
lindying, shimmying, hip swung glides
watching our grooves, showing precedent slides

He taught us:
  Buck and Bubbles,
              think through troubles,
  Nicholas Brothers,
               heed your family and not others,
  Bill Bojangles Robinson,
              though they steal your song
                    sing on.

Saved all his deft skill for us
Daddy could dance so many ways

He would lend me his grace:
letting me place small flat feet on his
and holding my hands, smiling,
would show me where to step

as if I could ever learn
to do it backwards and in heels
as if I could ever learn his strength.

A Simple Gift

- Imani Powell

I quietly peeked from behind the door, curious about the extraordinary orchestra of greens chopping, oil frying, and pots clanging. I knew that my dad was in the kitchen preparing a masterpiece and that our palates would soon be awakened by spicy curry. In my house as a child, I often came home to a pot of curry goat simmering to dark yellow perfection and a kitchen laced with exotic spices. Daddy always enjoyed cooking. It brings him joy. I remember him standing in his favorite overalls with a large knife in tow, rigorously dicing his onions and garlic with precision. The kitchen was off-limits when dad was in there doing his thing.

When Daddy would catch me looking on, knowing that I was anxious to find out what delicacy matched the enticing aroma that hailed from his kitchen, he'd lift my little body up over the large metal crock pot so that I could see the tiger prawns swimming in seas of red rice, spicy sausage, and red peppers staring back up at me. My daddy loves to eat and even more he loves to feed people—and especially me. I am his baby, his youngest child—his skinniest child, who shares his appetite for food. He still teases me about the way I could down two huge plates even faster than my older brother. I was his "little skinny bones with big feet." He always joked about where all my food went: "straight to your feet!" he would say. What can I say? When daddy's cooking, there is always room.

Daddy has a "foodie" worldview. For him, cities are marked not by famous landmarks and monuments, but by their delicatessens, restaurants and bakeries. On occasion, he'd pack the family in a car and drive us up to the coast of New England on a clam-chowder mission. We would stop along the coast in every state to sample the fresh fish and explore new delights like clams on a half-shell, clam strips with the belly and then without. As we dipped the crustaceans in tartar sauce or braved raw oysters, we were exploring the world through our palates.

New York City, where we lived was always an adventure. From the Italian ices from Corona's famous Lemon-Ice King to Middle Eastern Shwarma, dirty franks from Grey's Papaya Palace and Korean barbeque, I was being cultured. I learned of Moroccan Couscous, Dominican breakfasts of mashed green plantains and fried cheese and even of the joy of

White Castle hamburgers. He tried to expose us to as many different foods as possible, so that we would never be afraid to try new things, and would more importantly gain insight into the customs of other people. Dad believes that food is a common bond between people. He was preparing us to break bread with the world.

Dad is a welder with the union. He always made a decent living and provided for his family. He would work hard all day, leaving the house every morning at about 5:00 a.m. to return around 3:00 p.m. in oil-stained denim, a dirty Carthart jacket, construction boots, and a welder's cap tipped to the side. Accompanying his occasional third-degree burns and dirty fingernails was a box of Italian pastry from Biagio's, the bakery near his union hall. This was love. As tired as the man may have been, he worked to provide for us and lived to make us smile. A cannoli for Mom and me- that was our favorite. My brother, Daoud, got an éclair and Zawadi, my sister, a cream puff.

We all learned to appreciate small gifts. After the mortgage was paid, the car insurance was put aside; the long ride home from work on the Brooklyn Queens Expressway was endured. The schoolwork was finished, the house was clean, his burns were salved, we soothed the tediousness of the day with a simple gift—with the sweetness of chocolate, the tartness of tamarind-and there was no doubt in your mind that you were loved. It was a wonderful thing!

Through simple gifts, I was nurtured and cared for—I was shown that I was worthy and important. I learned that I deserved the sweetness and beauty that life has to offer and that we all do, and because I understand that, because I was shown that, I am able to share beauty and sweetness with the world—with both loved ones and strangers. I know how easy it is to make someone smile—to make someone feel important. It doesn't take a whole lot of money, effort or thought, just a little love, a Hershey's kiss, a Knish or some curry!

Imani and Dad

David Powell

Distant

EVERY ONCE IN AWHILE

"We are father and daughter and
because of our blood connection,
and our past, we stay in touch."

"...or maybe he lost my number."

"...we are spinning in opposite directions...orbiting in counter clockwise
revolutions around the same sun."

CHAPTER II

Distant: EVERY ONCE IN AWHILE

*H*ave you ever looked for something that you remember putting in a secure place, but when you needed it, it was no longer there? Then one day, it appears. You blame its absence on your forgetfulness or you accuse someone else of moving the item without your permission. When you finally retrieve the item, the reasons for its disappearance are no longer relevant, you're just glad to have it back in your possession.

Every once in awhile fathers are the disappearing item in a black woman's life. He was there at a time that she remembers; disappears at the time she wants to forget; and reappears at a time she can't explain. He is the revolving door in her life and with every sporadic departure, the black woman experiences some degree of "grief and loss," says Reverend Fox. In the end, it is her trust factor that is ultimately affected and she subconsciously wonders when every man in her life will one day pack his bags and disappear.

Some of the women in this chapter appreciate his return while others describe feelings of confusion, apprehension, and/or fear as they write him a letter, answer his phone call, meet him for dinner, or invite him into their homes for a short visit. They are full of questions about his inconsistency; however, no answer he gives will permanently extinguish the inquisitive flame. Their stories are to be continued until next time.

Tears for Fears

- Tina Smith Walker

Give that to the crack man
Vamp man
Cut-me-in-half-man
Bling bling man
Merry Christmas man
Give all that to the crack man
Little boy man
Mama daddy man
Empty shell man
Happy New Year man
Give that to the crack man

I met my father again in January 2001, after a 12 year hiatus. Our experiences had been as different as night and day; mine were spent in Illinois' educational facilities, his were in Illinois' correctional facilities. Nevertheless, we were both floating aimlessly through the "system," two strange, glowing orbs slightly off course.

The reunion was highly unlikely; much to my mother's chagrin he appeared at her 41st birthday celebration. Like the ghost of Christmas past, he rattled his shackles and manacles. I could envision my mother rubbing her wrists at the memory of hers. I didn't recognize him at first. The long Jheri curl of his youth was replaced with a gray, slightly balding crew cut. He hugged me tight, and whispered in my ear, "I love you once, I love you twice, I love you more than beans and rice." So he remembered. It was the last thing I'd ever said to him, written in a letter to the jail at 26th and California. I was about 11-years-old then.

We took up like old pals after that day, that day in January when my mother turned 41. I went to Narcotics Anonymous meetings with him; I never knew that my father had a heroin addiction older than I was. We played chess at my house; he met his three-year-old grandson. He called my husband his son.

Then the telephone calls started. The calls at twelve midnight; the calls that he was so sick, and the calls asking for money were endless. Money for shoes, money for medicine, money for food until his Link Card came in, money to give my aunt, money to take his girlfriend out on Father's Day. The calls to my husband's job, the calls to my cell phone, the endless string of messages on the voicemail. One night, there were 15 calls from the same pay phone, every 20 minutes. Never mind it was also the worst snowstorm of the year.

I had given my father almost a thousand dollars by the time I finally woke up. I told my husband to stop accepting the calls. My father was still using drugs, and he was also leaning on us. Each time I saw my father, a cash transaction took place and I was always on the withdrawal end. I cut off all communication for months.

Eventually, my spirit felt the need to speak. I called my father and invited him to a Sunday dinner; we would eat and play chess. He agreed and told me how much he missed me, how sorry he was about hurting me, and how much fun we would have. Sunday afternoon, I called my aunt's house. She informed me that my father had gone "outside." I waited for a return call; I didn't receive it until 11:00 p.m. In disgust, I let the voice mail pick it up. The message I heard left me in limbo; I was unsure whether to laugh or to cry. My father's voice was slurred with a numbing drug high. His words were spiked with venom. He yelled obscenities into the phone. He demanded money and commanded me to obey him, because he was my father. That was six months ago.

Last week my husband told me he received an urgent call. He said my father cried like a baby, begging to be a part of our lives again. I meditated on this information; I asked my soul how it felt. I asked for wisdom on what to do. I opened my heart wide and prayed for God to bless all our souls. It was all I could do for my father.

The tears meant little to me; I watched them course down his cheeks as he pleaded with my mother on bended knee, begging her to never leave him. I watched those tears roll like thunder as he promised to never drink whisky again. I watched those tears flow like purifying rains as he held ice and a towel to my mother's black eyes time and time again. I have been watching my daddy cry and beg my whole life. I just can't watch it anymore.

What will become of my father? What will become of me? We are eternally bonded; flesh of my flesh, blood of my blood. However we are spinning in opposite directions; we are two disconnected planets orbiting in counter-clockwise revolutions around the same sun. I open my heart wide, and pray for God to bless all our souls. It is all I can do.

A Childhood Stream of Consciousness

- Kathyrn Buford

I still do not know if she was actually scared. I was terrified. Beads of perspiration slid down the sides of my face. As I formed a tight fist in my right hand, my palm began to turn pale as my fingernails pierced through my small hands like daggers. I quickly opened my hand remembering that my brother had told me if I made a tight fist for more than one minute, my knuckles would burst through my skin. I had to open my hand; well over 30 seconds had elapsed.

As I unfolded my palm, he flung open the tattered car door. He was boiling on the inside and out. Even the sweat on his face was afraid to fall—it huddled together in the wrinkles of his forehead and especially close to the edges of his scalp for fear it might trickle down his nappy hair. He calmly told her to get out of the car. Flushed with fever, I abruptly turned my head forward. I wanted to concentrate on the clean spots of the dingy garage door, but instead, I turned my head to the right with insurgence.

He was steaming. Three strands of sweat courageously journeyed past the profile of his face. In the short time I spent attempting to focus on the unsoiled areas of my garage door something had happened. Something occurred that made her lay flat on the filthy cement. Now he had straddled her. He had always made it a point to make me wash my hands thoroughly after playing in the park or using the bathroom. Perhaps that is why the thin film of dirt underneath his fingernail seized my attention when he pointed his unsteady index finger in her face. I could not make out her face because I was too short to see past the seat cushion, but I knew that was where he was pointing. Yelling, he told her never to leave the house without telling him where she was going. I could see his neck muscles grinding as he bellowed. He screamed even louder than when he found out my brother had left his muddy shoes on the white carpet.

I wanted to do something then. I wanted to say something. When I remembered that my brother was in the back seat, I wanted him to act. I wanted to go back in time to the parking lot at the amusement park. I would have never lied to my mom about sitting in the back seat last. I should have known better than to lie. My dad had just preached about the obscene destiny of liars in Sunday School the day before. I accepted my fate in silence. I wanted to undo this scene, but I was paralyzed with insecurity and awe.

I hated watching what my mom called her "stories" on television. Sitting through an hour of insipid dialogue between wealthy white people was torture. It was second only to sitting through over two hours of insipid banter from a big black man with a bible and a donation basket. I could never follow the plot of the show. However, on one episode an attractive white man told some ugly woman that the eyes are the windows to the soul. The rest of the show repulsed me. I could not stomach seeing a man put his tongue in a woman's mouth, so I disdainfully placed my hands over my eyes. Out of morbid curiosity, I peered through them every half second.

I had to force myself to stop picturing the kissing scene, but the words of the white man were essentially wrapped around my brainstem. "The eyes are the window to the soul" would be my trademark; I decided it would be my catch phrase. I wanted to say it to adults, because every non-monosyllabic word I said was either cute or funny. However, I was too timid to talk. I remembered saying something clever that made my uncle laugh, yet it made my father send me to my room. I do not remember what I said, but I remember thinking that going to my room is better than getting a spanking. Just in case my dad did not recognize the "severity" of this punishment, I put on a sad face and somber disposition so he would think his penalty was sufficient.

It was not until fourth grade that I realized that there was nothing special about my potential catch phrase. My teacher ruined it. I cannot remember her name, because I only stayed at that school for about three months before we moved back to Oak Park. Some dumb white girl asked the teacher why her eyes were blue. My inane teacher evaded the question by talking about German people and blurting out, "The eyes are the windows to the soul." Stupid bitch. On the long bus ride, in the privacy of their homes, and at school the following days, eager children were parroting my catch phrase. My signature saying was coming out of the mouths of idiots.

I had no reason to get as mad as I did. That saying was, is, and will always be hollow, because it does not make sense. The eyes have nothing to do with the soul. They are merely puppets that the brain manipulates to see. Moreover, the brain and the soul are two separate entities. My soul is going to hell, because my brain does not understand why I have to read the bible, pray, and go to church. My brain, on the other hand, gets a nicer resting place. God would have made sure of that because he and I did not get along.

God was increasingly dividing me from my father who kept instructing me to love God more than anything, including him. He was the perfect example of how to lead my religious life. He put God first, church second, my brother and I third and what was left of his deteriorating relationship with my mother, last. I grew as numb to their arguments as I did to the idea of God's power. I knew God existed and I understood the rules He wanted me to follow. Most importantly He wanted me to be truthful, to not steal, and to have any gods before Him.

I rationalized lying, stealing, and putting television before prayer and the Bible. If God wanted me to obey Him, He would not have made His rules so fun to break. I still prayed at night for forgiveness. I knew that since my prayers were completely insincere God was not even listening, but because my dad had been forcing me to pray every night, I did so habitually. Eventually, I just accepted the fact that I was not a good person by Christian standard at least. I could not wash my hands of my amusing evil deeds. I told myself that hell could not be too bad. It was not hard for me to accept a fate in the squalid pit of hell, but it was rather difficult to look my father in the eye and pretend to be a perfect Christian daughter.

If anything, the hands, not the eyes are the windows to the soul. The same hands that leafed through storybook pages, prayed over people at my church, and helped me cross the street had stabbed me in the back when he pushed my mother flat on the filthy cement.

I loved to play go fish with him. He made me laugh when he would change the rules of the game so he could win. Whenever he said that an ace could count as a three, I would chuckle and say, "Daddy, stop." He would eventually succumb to my pleas and fix the game so I would win. That night, before he had finished screaming down at her, I was silently yelling, "Daddy, stop."

rock daddy

- Barbara Lewis

the mosaic of his words
broken into variegated shards
pushed through the wire
spliced into my dream of
true paternal rock.
baby, he stammered, i overextended
myself and have to take back your
birthday present. can't afford it
now. but next year.
cracked the door to hand
over the sewing machine
down the path he walked
off balance with the weight
watched his back fade
out the yard
across the street
around the corner
and my marrow knew
why all these years mother
had called him "more flash than cash"

JAILBIRD'S WING:
Poems for my Father
- Meredith Bloedorn

SPRING

Despite Manhattan's concrete walls
And lack of greenery
The first whisper of spring
Has found me yet again

I walk through a jungle of steel & stone
While in my mind's eye
It is the damp forest ground
That absorbs my step
I touch every flower
Caress each new leaf
And wonder
As my eyes open to the harsh reality
Of my true surroundings
Is it the same for you?

Behind bars
Another season passes
Slowly bringing you closer to a day
When the gates will birth you
(like all spring's children)
Fresh and new into this world

I see you on that day
Walking
Never looking back
Your stride steady
Your head high
Until you see that first blossom

You reach
Grasping with all your might
Pulling it close
You breathe deeply
Then fill the top buttonhole
Of your faded blue shirt
(that same shirt from so long ago)

I see you on that day
You are free
Standing tall
And wearing that flower
As if to say
"Life, oh blessed life"

Visiting Day or They Steal Color

Everything is white:
Your uniform
The state walls
The vast fields of cotton

Tears and the brightness
Dazzle my eyes
But I hold back an ocean
With the strength of a daughter
On visiting day

Pride holds me erect
You know I will not falter
Under the gaze of prison guards
Removing all metal (like armor?)
From my body
I silently promise
To let the tears stream
When you finally walk from these doors
To paint every color on the wind
To never wear white

Shadow Father

I gave you a dashiki wear
I laced beads in your half-breed hair
I gave you eyes as dark as night
I made you rainbow wings for flight
I fashioned broad shoulders for you
To carry me
I cried at night because you would never be
More than a shadow, Father

Hope In Arkansas or Free Tommy Lee

The dry air
Had me spitting dust
And more

I played Alice Coltrane
Crossing from Tennessee to Arkansas
The sun set purple red
As I wove the story of our life

Through cotton in bloom
Like clouds
But opposite
Lying on the ground
Not moist
Sucking the air

It was beautiful
But I could feel the danger
How this place can sap you
The grit in my teeth
Like life here

Signs for the state prison
Point beyond the fields
I get down on my knees
And look to the red stained sky for answers

Getting none
I close my eyes
Seeing in negative
The clouds in the sky
Now brilliant white
The cotton   state walls   and your uniform
Now tinged with Sunset
The blood of our lives

From hands always holding on
Reaching through barbed wire time
From being a daughter alone here
From being a man in a cage

Touching earth
I gather the strength
To keep making this blanket
A warm and honest story

A bird takes off from the pattern
Riding an invisible wave of hope south west
On the wind I hear its song
"Freeeeeeeee
Free Tommy Leeeeeee"

The Father I Now Know

- Chante` Bowns

No matter what we say, no matter what we do, no matter how much we deny it, there's always a place in our hearts saved just for fathers. This place reserved for fathers continues in our hearts for as long as we live. Maybe your father has not come to redeem this place in your heart, so you allow another person or object to occupy that place. The truth of the matter is, that no matter how much you try to fill the place you "saved just for daddy," there still comes a time when that place will again become an empty void that longs to be filled.

I think that was the way it was with me. My father was absent after I turned ten-years-old. This was unusual, because I was used to him being an active part of my life, and I didn't understand what was happening when he stopped coming around. After my father left, I began remembering how much quality time he would spend with me. We would go to the park, shop for Easter clothes, and even visit my grandmother on his side of the family. I loved those times and I longed to have them back. I wanted the times when I was "daddy's baby girl" to return.

To keep my mind off the hurt I felt, I started to fill that place with whatever and whomever I could. I consumed myself with reading, writing, church, school activities, or just hanging out with my friends. I no longer worried about when I would hear from or see my father, nor did I ever allow anyone else to see me hurting from the pain that his absence caused. However, no matter how much I tried to lose myself in life, that void would always become empty again.

I tricked myself into believing that my father had a good explanation for never being around. I would tell myself that he was probably working hard to save enough money for my college education or maybe he lost my number, because those lies made me feel better.

Soon it seemed that I had forgotten about my father not being there and I started to think about him less and less. Everyone would ask me when was the last time I had seen my father, as if I could actually recall the last day I had seen him. My response would always be "on Thanksgiving" or "just a few weeks ago, and look he gave me two dollars, whoopee!"

As the years progressed, I was becoming a mature young lady, and it hit me that my father had no part in it. I decided to do something about it. First, I called my father's mother to get his number at home. She was very reluctant about giving me his personal information. "For goodness sakes," I thought. I was his child. Instead, she told me that she would tell him that I had called for him.

My father got back in touch with me as soon as he heard that I called for him. It kind of erased all the hurt, pain, and neglect that I had been feeling for years in that moment when he called me. He mentioned that he knew I was graduating from 8th grade and he offered to pay for my outfit. I thanked him and told him that I loved him, knowing that I wanted more from him than a graduation outfit.

Two days after I talked with my father, he showed up at my house. I didn't even know how to greet him. I wanted to hug him, but my mind told me not to, instead he grabbed me and hugged me and told me in his fatherly voice, "Don't act like you don't know who I am." Little did he know, it wasn't an act. I really didn't know who he was. I told him that I was the valedictorian of my class and I invited him to my graduation, but he declined. His decline didn't faze me, because I knew he was proud of me and he wanted to be there to see me walk across the stage with pride, but his inner-man would not allow the guilt of our past relationship to let go forever.

His absence at my graduation didn't stop me from trying to reel my father into my life with love. In fact, when he didn't call me on November 17, 2000, my sixteenth birthday, I took the initiative of calling him myself. It was my sixteenth birthday and the gift of his love was the thing that mattered most to me on that day. I didn't need him to buy me clothes or give me money. I was beyond the stage of accepting money as proof of someone's love for me. I was ready for a relationship with my father and nothing would stop me from doing what it took to get it.

Today I speak to my father every so often. He comes to visit me at work, calls, and says that he loves me, and when he doesn't say it, I still know it's in his heart and mind. Even though my father and I rarely see or hear from each other, we are so much alike that I know he has part of me in his life. Lord knows I have thought so much about what would become of father and me. As long as I have known my father, I think he's been distant in some type of way. I guess I just didn't see it when I was younger, but he shows his love for his "baby girl" in his own little way, every once in awhile.

CEREMONIES

- Sharon R. Amos

uncertain about college stuff freshman year you gave me fifteen dollars to buy books/wondered why I stayed up all night studying and writing papers/told me to buy a dress not bell bottom jeans that made me look like some hippie/I became the first in the family to earn a degree/I wanted you to watch me walk across the stage/for you/for my mother/for all those who hadn't/ didn't you want to see me take a giant step toward life/away from home/is that why you didn't come/so you wouldn't have to/so you could keep your baby girl?

he asked you for my hand and you granted it/fathers do give their daughters away at weddings/ wearing timeshare tuxedos and patent shoes/didn't you want to walk down the aisle/my eyes brimming with tears/ is that why you stayed away/afraid you would drink too much again/you didn't want to risk embarrassing me/is that why you didn't come/so you wouldn't have to/so you could keep your baby girl?

summer arrived and so did your grandson/a year later I watched you play with him/you laughed when he climbed in the cabinets with the pots and pans/with me you talked about your life and how you'd always loved me/fits of coughing wracked your body/the doctors asked how long you'd had the pains/I tried bargaining with God/but you slipped away so silently/I became the reluctant one/who couldn't bear to see you/who didn't want to say goodbye/it's your baby girl/daddy/still your baby girl /daddy.

Reckoning

- Raquel Rivera

I pace and wait—just outside
The palisade, just beyond the sod
Lawn purpled with rows of cabbage
Flowers—for a pauper's meal
Of stale saltines and chamomile
Tea to lull a restive stomach.

Swiss chalet-styled tenements,
Pine straw and twine reindeer
Make cheap art to decorate
Poverty's taut stomach.
Suburbia is not immune,
Even my voice is affected.

Ruminating this, our shared history.
Now I am an adult, but a child
Remembers how you would return
Home from the road, the Buick
Tucked beneath the carport,
A warm hood the signpost for hush.

Hush, mustn't let you hear me
Grumbling. I open the gate, walk, press
Finger to the bell, and beat down
All misgivings before untying
The scarf looped 'round my neck. A geste of mores
I don once, weekly. No need to pretend, I am

The silken noose, the chafing daughter you endure
Each Sunday. Father, I've come to tell you
How a man's bones want laths,

Deteriorating support for this two-story
Debtor's prison. While you were absent
Your children filed away. Silently

Running off with your money
In our heads. We may not have
Business degrees, yet masquerading
Codpieces between the talented tenth
Made us creative. Oh, how will you explain?
These silver spoons you've crafted!

Don't swallow hard, we've chosen
This life, to live simply.
Your sacrifices afforded us
This luxury. We still have
The tarnished gifts you gave,
Our one material possession.

We have built display cases
To house our valuable reminder:
Conspicuous consumption
Left us hungry to know you.
Hurry, Father, open the door.
The air is unkind out here.

Wet flurries fringe my hair,
A progression of lit windows
Move through evening. Locks turn,
Warily. Night offers it first star.
A plangent voice calls "Who's there?"
I summon my voice in answer

Estrangement

- Linda Susan Jackson

With a jelly glass full of lemonade,
I stand at the curb, three sandy
haired braids, hanging.

Everyday in white anklet socks, scalloped
edges stuffed into oxblood leather Mary
Janes, anticipation roots me to the curb.

Forces my head left/right. No arms reach out
to me. No hands pull me up on Daddy's shoes.

Dressed in yellow today, yesterday baby
blue, I expect to see myself in his eyes.

My need masquerades as casual pride.
I won't move beyond yesterday's
disappointment, dropping like a guillotine.

A Birthday Card from My Father

- Opal Palmer Adisa

Today I received a birthday card from my father and it puts a smile on my face. My father hasn't sent me a card in years. Nor have I sent him any. As I read the fatherly affections printed in the card, my heart flutters, light as a butterfly. I turn the card over in my hand, admiring the deep blue sky of the landscape scene. I read the letter he includes, asking details about my life. I wonder what receiving a birthday card from my father this year means? I place it on my desk and glance at it, wishing it would reveal my father's thoughts to me. He actually remembered my birthday, I say out loud, and rise from the chair. I pace the floor in my office, and speak to the walls as if I'm addressing my father.

Are you willing to see me as the woman I have become? Are you willing to treat me as an adult and respect my reservations as much as you are demanding that I respect yours? Are you able to call it truce and allow us to enjoy the rest of the time and the life we both have? I want us to find that place, and real soon, daddy, I add.

I sit back down to write my father a letter of acknowledgement, but my pen stalls. I hesitate to write Dear Daddy; it doesn't sound right in my head. I try Dear Orlando, and although that is his name, it doesn't have the emotional charge I want. How should I address him? What feels comfortable? I stand up and pace some more, ruminating inside my head. Why is this still so difficult for me? What answers don't I have that I want from him? Do I still need and want to hear him say, I'm sorry I wasn't there for you all those years, but I loved you always.

I tell myself again that I don't expect an apology from him, but a persistent voice says, "You deserve one. He owes it to himself, to you, to his ancestors, and to the world to make peace with his adult children before he dies." The stubborn voices quiet and I chime: "that's all I want, to make peace, for you to realize that I am no longer the little girl you left, who cried, Daddy. I am a woman. And if we are to have a relationship, it has to be as one adult to another, trying to find our way back to each other to connect in the present moment."

The images of you that are stored inside my head are snippets, small glasses of sweetsop juice. You are laughing, drinking, and joking with friends on the veranda. You are walking around the yard in only shorts, gardening, firm, no fat, and the color of cocoa. You put me on your lap and allowed me to steer your car when I was four-years-old. I almost steered it into the canal.

You wrecked your car while traveling to Kingston. The whisper is that you were drunk. I remember when you came home from the hospital. You had to be fed with a straw, because you had injured your jaws as well as broken your leg. It was a miracle you had survived. As I stood at the entrance of the room watching my mother spoon-feed you, I whimpered, afraid to come close, my pain and fear trapped in my stomach, yours bound to you in the cast on your leg.

You did not say anything to Dawn and me when Mommie disappeared one day. We didn't know where she was, until she returned a month later and packed all our belongings. That day we left is like a wasp sting on my arm. You were standing on the veranda as Mommie, Dawn and I piled in the truck with all our belongings. You watched us leave. You didn't beg us to stay; you didn't wave goodbye.

A few months later, you came to get us while Mommie was at work, but the maid called her. Mommie came home during the middle of the day, with a policeman who told you that you couldn't take us; we had to stay with our mother. My sister wanted to go with you, but she also wanted to stay with Mommie. I said I wasn't going with you.

You came to my birthday party after we had moved again, this time into our own home. Everyone left, but you refused to go. Mommie begged you to leave. Finally, she locked the door and left you sitting on the veranda in the dark.

Every Sunday, during the summer weeks we stayed with you. You took us to Gun Boat Beach before it was officially open. We climbed over the gate. The water was usually chilly, but one at a time, you took Dawn and me on your back and swam way out of sight. While I waited on the shore for you to return, I wondered if you would be able to swim the returning distance. You were a spot in the water I prayed wouldn't disappear.

We stayed those weeks in your tiny apartment that you shared with that woman and her child Patsy. We had dinner when you came home from work. We had to sit quietly without resting our elbows on the table. We always ate with knife and fork. Sunday afternoons we went for drives. Dawn and I and Pasty sat in the back of your Morris in our Sunday dresses with matching ribbons in our hair. You narrated our drive through the city. I was eight-years-old when your father died. I hardly knew him.

The day of his funeral, after you and the other male relatives dressed him for burial, you came and got Dawn and me from in the yard where we were playing with cousins we had never met before. Your palms were wet and warm like a damp cloth as you led us into the cold, dank room where grandpa laid. Then you lifted and passed, first me, then Dawn, over grandpa's body.

I would often go into the room where grandpa laid covered with ice, to peek at him, and to see if he would get up. But he never did, not even when I took a handful of ice-mint from the sweetie jar on the counter, in the adjacent shop area. People remarked what a brave child I was, not being afraid of the dead.

A few years later, Aunt Lyn, your sister, died. She never made it home from the airport after returning from America. At her funeral, I remember thinking your face looked like a hard, dry coconut still in its shell; you seemed vexed with the world and I couldn't think of anything to say to make you laugh.

Finally, I remember a party at Nanny, your mother's house where you arrived very late with a woman. Although Mommie looked beautiful in a shiny blue dress, neither of you spoke to each other. How could that be and you were married, I wondered. People whispering about you at the party and I had to keep moving away to not hear what they were saying. My stomach kept tying up in knots and I had to press on it.

After that, whenever I asked about my father and why he didn't come to see us anymore, Mommie said he had moved to America. At first I would sit on the steps and listen for the postman's bicycle bell. When I heard it ringing, I ran to the gate and took the mail for him. There was never any letter with my name on it. Daddy didn't write, but I wrote to him when my playmates in the neighborhood chanted,

"You don't have a daddy! You don't have a daddy!"

"Yes I do!" I shouted back, tears stinging my cheeks. I ran home, tore a page out my exercise books and wrote:

Dear Daddy:
Please come and visit. My friends think I don't have a daddy, and I do. They are so stupid. Please come so I can introduce you to them. Once they meet you, they will know that I have a wonderful daddy.

Your very best daughter,
mus-mus

I even signed it with your nickname for me, but I never mailed it. I didn't know your address. After a while, I no longer listened for the postman, but every so often I wondered where you were, what you were doing, if you missed me? I knew you had to be hurt about not coming to my birthday party or sending me a card. Then I thought you must be angry with me for choosing to live with Mommie instead of you. That is why you didn't come to see me anymore. That is why you didn't write. I tucked you away, but would pull you out every so often.

I sent you invitations to my first dance performance and I even wrote you when Mommie said I was too young for boyfriends. You never replied to any of my letters. You never called. You never visited. You never sent birthday cards? You were not present at most of the major or minor events in my life, and I needed you, wanted reassurance that you loved me. I ached to know where you were. I desired my daddy, but you were simply not there. And it hurt. And I cried.

Some days, I sat under the Ackee tree and cried from missing you. Some mornings I woke up, and realized I was crying in my sleep from dreaming about you.

Dear Daddy:
This is an SOS. Where are you? Please come and visit. I just need to see you. I feel so alone as if no one understands me, but I know that you would. Come soon.

Your needy daughter with love,
Opal

I didn't write you after that, and I convinced myself that I didn't have a daddy. You were not dead, just erased, your place covered over with stones like the ones we piled to mark where we buried my dog, Brownie.

When we relocated to New York, six years later after your alleged migration, I secretly believed I would run into you on the street or that you would track me down, ask for my forgiveness and say how you have been looking for me. You would call me Mus-Mus and tell me how much you have missed me.

A few weeks after my college graduation, I arrived home, and Mommie casually said, "There is a letter on the bookcase addressed to you and Dawn from your father." I think I paused. I am sure I must have had some response. I remember taking up the letter and looking to make sure it was indeed addressed to me. I saw your return name and address, sucked my teeth, and placed the letter right back on the bookcase.

"It's too late," I said as I headed up the stairs for my room.

My sister read the letter as soon as she came home. A few days later, alone at home, the letter still on the bookcase, I took out the pages and read it.

It was a "Dear Daughters" letter, as if we had been in contact with you all along, as if you hadn't just dropped out of our life without a word. I threw it in the trash.

At Mommie's encouraging, after my sister called and spoke with you, we took the long train ride to White Plains and visited with you. Your wife, the woman you used to live with when we visited during the summers before you left, hugged us like long-lost and now returned daughters. Her daughter Patsy, now grown, the same little girl we used to play with, was my sister, just a year and a half younger than me. That meant she was born while you were still married to Mommie, while you lived as husband and wife. All this time and I didn't know that she was my sister. My tongue lay heavy in my mouth.

I visited my father once more before I returned home to Jamaica. I promised I would write and I did; the kind of vapid, here-is-what-I-am doing-obligatory letter every three months. I kept hoping that he would fill in the blanks about his absence, but he never did.

When my second child was born, my husband and I went visiting relatives back East, and I took my family to meet my father. I was prompted to write this letter to my father, which I did mail.

Dear Orlando:

In the most ideal time and place that live in my imagination, you and I grew up together. You watched me mature; I witnessed you age. We enjoyed a close, loving relationship. I would tell you about the men I fancied, the man I would marry, and you would advise. Mostly, you encouraged me to be myself, to follow my dreams relentlessly and to live with integrity and honesty, always. And if like now, we live in separate states, we would call each other weekly. We would write to each other regularly, and you would tell me stories about your life as a boy and then as a young man.

My head would be full of you, and I would carry you around in my heart, always. We would visit yearly and while my children run around and mess up your neat home or fumble through your old, mildewed photo albums, you and I would talk over a cup of tea or stroll through your garden. Our arms would be hooked, and we would talk and laugh and lean on each other, happy that we are father and daughter.

Peace,

Opal

My father and I never discussed the letters I sent him. I seldom called him. We don't have that intimate relationship. We are father and daughter and because of our blood connection, and our past, we stay in touch.

The phone rings and I am brought back to the present. I glance at the card on my desk. I decide it is time to visit you and bring my youngest to meet you.

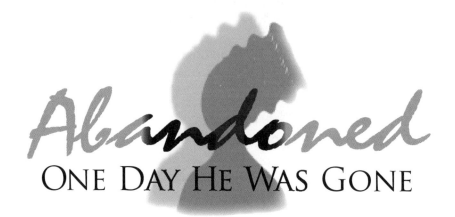

Abandoned

ONE DAY HE WAS GONE

"His absence taught me how to appreciate other's presence and his inability to be there for me has made me stronger."

"... the one thing a girl like me needs to hear from her daddy...is that she did not run him away."

"... Michael was too apathetic to fulfill his role and allowed other things to take the place of fatherhood."

CHAPTER III

Abandoned: ONE DAY
HE WAS GONE

*T*alk shows, daytime and nighttime dramas, and Hollywood scandals are notorious for giving stage to men leaving their wives, or glamorizing a break up with their girlfriends. The media thrives on dysfunctional relationships. We are often left despising the man and pitying the woman. However, we rarely expend our emotions on the children who are caught in the middle. Sonya Green, contributor for Newomen.com's Life Stories says, "Deep within us is a need to love our parents. We need to know that above all else, our parents love us. Without this, there is a 'soul emptiness,' a disconnect from ourselves." A young girl, who has known her father and then one day made to wonder about his whereabouts, carries fears of abandonment into future relationships with all men. A study done on Black Women Health and Social Policy Development (2001), acknowledges that for black women some of the issues rooted in high rates of depression, suicide, and substance abuse are experiences with abandonment. What is the baggage that black women carry when one day "daddy" is gone?

These soul searching writings attempt to answer that question with candor and sincerity. The voices describe stories of fond memories of their time together, anger over broken promises, blame for his failure to protect them from incest, confusion on his disappearance, acceptance of the void he has left in their lives, and resolve to love him in spite of the disconnect.

Faith[1]

- Niama Williams

*t*he check has not come yet and i'm trying real hard not to lose faith in you. the check has not come yet and my heart sinks as i look at the mail in my hand. i think maybe it was those same post office bitches who stole my *new yorkers* and occasionally forget we have mailboxes and just scatter the mail all over the foyer floor.

the check has not come yet and i'm trying real hard to remember how delighted and surprised your voice sounded when i called the other day to inquire after it. i never realized before i decided stubbornly and on my own to love you and how your voice changes once you realize it's me on the phone.

whenever i call you at home you always answer with a sharp tinge of "who the hell are you and why are you bothering me at home?" in your voice. but once i say hello i can almost see your whole demeanor change. you almost always laugh, and i hear the smile as you say, "hohoho and how are you?" i never noticed this dramatic change in your voice until i stopped holding my breath every time i dialed your number, until i voluntarily came out from under the mama mojo.

and even that wasn't totally her fault. we both know she had a right to be angry and hurt. i was never so surprised as when i heard you admit that you knew you'd ruined her life. i was so stunned by your honesty, your obviously long-term acceptance of your guilt; it almost over-shadowed the thunder of your subsequent pronouncement.

see, the one thing a girl like me needs to hear from her daddy, the daddy she has always doted on, is that she did not run him away.

you left and then were busy building your new life while i was enduring my formative years. i think maybe you couldn't stand to know what my brothers were doing to me in their anger at your absence.

i think a part of you still doesn't want to know. i know now that had you been with us it would never have happened because you wouldn't have allowed it. somehow i don't fault you for that. somehow i know there are certain things even a parent, maybe especially a parent, can't bear to hear from their child.

but what i do thank you for is that honest answer. it was part lie by omission, but i recognized the honest part and that was enough. it was a long and tawdry road that led up to the night i asked you why you left; a road whose final turn was cinched by the man i fell in love with. he was an incredibly loving man who turned my life upside down. of course he didn't want me, we all have our patterns, but he was kind enough to make me realize as he left that love was possible, that men could have a function in my life, that there was a reason for the phenomenon of "couple." what i realized after loving this man was that i had smothered him, then proceeded to drive him as far away as possible. by then i knew the pattern, could trace it right to its sources.

there was no use in talking to her, but i knew that night as my lips formed the question that i had to know you, and how you really felt about me, before i could love a man without sending him screaming in the other direction.

so i asked.

and you answered.

i left, you said, because it had gotten to the place where i couldn't even say good morning without an argument starting. i was unhappy and so i left.

life together had just become unlivable. how well i knew mornings like that with her. moments when it was absolutely impossible to say the right thing. i knew that symptom too, because i had used it on my friend.

though i didn't think about it that night, there was another part to the truth. you were stepping out and had been for awhile. but in that kernel of what you did say, lay a lifting of the chains for me. the talkative, inquisitive five-year-old who adored you was no longer the one who had driven you out of the house. the one whose ability to say anything she was told, had continually shocked and embarrassed you. the one who was repeatedly told you already had one foot out the door before she was even conceived.

your one small kernel of truth may not put the lie to all of that, but it did put the lie to one important thing: my guilt at running you off. all of a sudden i could give back to my brothers their responsibility for knocking my head against the wall and ordering me to pull down my pants. i couldn't blame you and i couldn't blame her, but i could certainly blame them. they were teenagers and i was not the one who had brought their hearts to the edge of breaking.

listening to your one kernel of truth i was able to let the guilt and shame and responsibility go. i was able to stop holding my breath where you were concerned. i was able to believe the smile on your face in the photo where you're showing me off to your friends.

the check has not come yet, but i understand now why frederick douglass and a photograph of a toddlin me are the only two portraits on the wall of your very professional office.
i laughed when you said you told ignorant white folks that the portrait of douglass was a picture of your grandfather. i didn't tell you then, but my heart almost burst when you said the little girl next to him was a little girl named leslie.

so the check has not come yet and i'll probably call you today, sunday, to roast those post office bitches who stole my *new yorkers* and probably my check. monday i'll go to sixteenth and thompson with my "black-woman-from-the-ghetto-clothes" on. cause one thing you taught me is that niggas are not always reliable. the other was that you loved me.

An Open Letter to My Dad

- J. Victoria Sanders

You were always inconsistent
doin somethin & then bein sorry
beatin my heart to death
talkin bout you sorry
-- Ntozake Shange

It is so true that people show you who they are when you first meet them. I haven't met anyone who has proved that better than you.

When I was 17, I was looking for a daddy to fill the void in my life. Did you keep the fashion sketches, pictures, and five-page letter I sent to you? You didn't respond for a year. I poured my life out over several pages, sent the letter, and counted the days until I heard from you again. I didn't want to include you in the ranks of stereotypical black men who shun paternal responsibility. Were you resentful that I was in boarding school with rich girls who flaunted the wealthy love of their fathers? Maybe it was my fault. Maybe I waited too long to ask you why you left me when I was so young. Maybe you just didn't know what to say.

I wanted security. I thought that after years of intermittent drama with mom that you couldn't have anything worse to offer me. At least you could complete the puzzle I was to myself, since everyone knows whether or not you want to be like your parents, you inherit characteristics from both unconsciously. I knew what my mother had given me—endurance, faith, and extreme optimism—but there was no telling how much you would add to my life.

If you had been around, maybe I could have avoided homelessness, constant moving, and poverty. I didn't want to blame you for my childhood tribulations; after all, they made me who I am. So did your silence. Every Father's Day, every Christmas, every birthday, I thought of you. Where is he? Is he celebrating? My mom said you were tall and wide. She said you looked like Barry White. Whenever I saw someone who fit the description, I gave him the look—Are you my father? It never occurred to me that if you wrote me back or if you called that I would be confronted with my anger towards you; that I might not be able to forgive you this lifetime.

You just didn't want to be bothered. I was thinking like the average abused child that it was my fault you didn't write back. Maybe you were hurt that I hadn't written earlier. But I was hurt too. I decided, after weeks of mulling over how to get you to respond, that the passive, sweet approach might have invoked some disgust in you. I am a black woman to my heart, needing a call and response relationship with everyone I invite into my life—but somehow my call to you had been disconnected. I wrote you another letter.

I was about to graduate from high school. I was on my way to Vassar College. Look where I was! Did you think I needed you? Pseudo-Superwoman rage spilled all over one ripped piece of notebook paper. I cursed you for rejecting me with your silence. "Fuck you if you think I can't make it the rest of the way without you," I wrote. When you called, I knew your voice like I know the rhythm of my breath. "Hi," you said in a low monotone. "It's your father." I had no idea what to say.

You seemed to think I would curse you out, or ask you where you had been for 17 years. I was so happy to hear your voice that I didn't think about the questions in the back of my mind. I just wanted to talk and get to know you. Nothing more or less.

As I said goodbye, you hung up before I had a chance to say, "I Love You." Maybe that was a sign. Intuition told me to leave the situation alone. I had heard your voice. I knew you had heard what I had to say. But I kept pressing for more. You seemed to call at least once a week from then on, because you were happy to have the daughter in your life that you had never known.

The first time I saw you at my high school graduation, you told the story about seeing me when I was a toddler. You said I kept you at bay, like I knew you were going to leave and never come back. I was only three, but you still held me responsible for my reaction, even then.

You towered over me like a demigod, resembling a black Santa Claus. Your thick black beard covered a face that was oblong like mine. Your eyes expressive but small, and your feet were huge, another trait I inherited. I waited for you to say, "Congratulations," but it never happened. You looked like you couldn't wait to leave. I stole glances at your face, but it was a canvas of hidden thoughts.

I didn't get the hint. You never wanted me to be apart of your life or your family. Yes, you fathered me. No, you weren't absolutely sure I was your baby. You simply tolerated this new development in your life. I was so thirsty for a "normal" relationship with you that I brushed your nonchalance aside. I was busy thinking of the future. I could call you on those nights when I felt like killing myself and you would list all the things I had to live for. The day I married my soul-mate, you would walk me down the aisle.

It was easy to have pipe dreams about our future, because I still lived with mom. We lived in a bare apartment in the Bronx; mattresses piled against walls for beds, clothes in big heaps inside our closets, because we couldn't afford dressers.

My books lined the floor, stretched out like a multi-colored accordion at the base of the bedroom walls. Our meals consisted of canned goods from church pantries. The love between us was marked by relentless hunger, sporadic anger, and blunt confusion, but you didn't care about that. You only gave me what you thought I needed-—which were all things that I asked you for. As long as I asked you nicely, you said.

At the time though, we had a few things in common besides big feet and long legs: our humorous and sarcastic confusion about my mother's sanity, a loose relationship with God, love of privacy, and a quiet curiosity about which one of us would be the first to test the boundaries of our overdue connection.

I was doomed with you from the very beginning. I needed at least one parent I could depend on, and you used that to your advantage. My college bills became your unspoken responsibility and you stopped speaking to me for several months. No phone calls, no letters, no nothing. You were annoyed that I asked you to pay tuition and mad that I just assumed that you could take care of me. You didn't think that giving me six hundred dollars in cash when I didn't even ask for it was reason enough for me to assume that you weren't suffering financially.

And as if I wasn't vulnerable enough, you scoffed at me when I told you I was born to be a writer. That was the defining line that separated us forever, and I even brushed that off. There was nothing you could have said to me that would have hurt me more. But instead of trusting in God as I had done before I met you, I only tried hard to make you proud of me; to love me, whether I was a writer, a klutz, or a sentimental girl who just couldn't figure out how to be a daughter.

Everything about us felt wrong. I was in the throes of your psychological abuse, wondering why I wasn't good enough for you to love me. Like most of the men I had loved wholeheartedly and intimately, you could only love me on your terms: from a distance, conditionally, and unfaithfully.

As a college graduate, I was positive that the tide would change. When I left your house, I said I would come back to visit, even when you said I should move everything out of your house. You gave me a solid gold watch with diamonds circling its face the day I graduated from college. The man who handed me a thousand dollars, told me, "The ATM machine is now closed," and said in the same breath that I had no choice but to succeed.

And only now, thousands of miles away from you, can I understand what transpired between us. I stole your crystal ball during one of my vacations from college. And instead of giving it back, I kept it. In a drunken rage, I hurled it out of my dorm room window. In my soul, I felt that there was no future between us. I was so tired of being hurt that I transformed my pain into teeming anger.

In my soul, I knew that I would rather have a hobo on the street walk me to the altar than you. I didn't like you, let alone love you, but I have decided to make peace with the fact that God chose you to play a part in my creation. He used you to make me feel secure, even though I wasn't. He used you to teach me that no matter how much you care about someone or how much you think you need him or her, nothing can change a hardened heart.

When I called to keep the lines of communication open, you said you didn't want me to call you anymore. Only then did I realize that I had given more of myself to pleasing you than I had ever given to myself. Now that I know that I gave all the energy I could to loving and understanding you, I am at complete peace. I can only hope that before you die you learn that you can love someone without hurting her too. Real love should not hurt. I pray that you learn that money cannot and will not ever make up for lost time. But most of all, I hope that no one ever makes it as hard for you to love them as you made it for me to love you.

Only God knows if I will see you again. As the holidays approach, I have vague memories of the two years we spent as "father" and "daughter." No more long talks about destiny or books or what true love is. No more tense arguments about money and sanity and what the future will hold. I believe God is omnipotent, and does not take one person out of your life without putting another soul in the empty space. He stepped up to fill the void I thought you could fill. He is the Daddy that I searched for and never found until you were but a blotch on my memory.

Thank you for all that you have and haven't done for me. Without our drama, I would not be the woman I am. We met and laughed and fumed with each other for a short time for a reason. Now I understand that there are too many kinds of love to qualify them all with mere words or gestures. Toni Morrison once wrote, "Thin love ain't no love at all." I pray you find thick, encompassing love, and embrace it, before it is too late. In the meantime, I will love you from a distance.

Unconditionally,
Joshunda Victoria Sanders

Fear #2

- Michelle R. Smith

i asked for you on my thirteenth birthday
my sixteenth my eighteenth & my twenty-first

for a sign
a smoke signal from your distant cave
a star from your perch in heaven

something to let me know that you remembered
& that you cared

years become blinks
rapid & unconscious
& every time you open your eyes
the world is unfamiliar

the only thing you recognize is the faces
no matter how sunken or wizened
they have become

& i keep looking for yours
i keep waiting
i keep wanting
you to come back for me
to show me what i was
& show me what i will be

& i shouldn't
because it is obvious that the years have made you
forgetful
have buried me under the sediment of lost time

you know what you have taught me, father
in your long, cold absence
in your silence
with our aborted life?

that i am the kind of girl that is easily left behind

Superhero

- Mary Ruth Theodos

An older woman once told me, "Mary Ruth, you will never fully be comfortable being Black as long as you live in America." I have spent the past eight years of my life exploring that statement and have yet to come up with a solution. Yet, I do know this. I will never be fully comfortable with the fact that my father was too busy watching his Superhero on television, The Incredible Hulk, that he was moments away from missing my birth. That should have been my first clue about my father, Michael. He wanted to be there, and he wanted to be my Superhero, but Michael was too apathetic to fulfill his role and allowed other things to take the place of fatherhood.

People tell me that I am lucky, because since the age of six I have had a stepfather who raised me. I am lucky because Gene has been much more than a stepfather. He has been my daddy. He is the one who helped me with homework or drove me to ballet class, and I know that even though we are not connected by blood, he loves me as if I was his own. But it is not the same. He is not Black, and cannot offer himself to me as a positive role model for my culture.

Others tell me that I have God as a father figure in my life, and yes, that is true. I do have my faith. God is a father to me in many ways. He created me and loves me unconditionally. But it is not the same. God is not tangible, and cannot offer Himself to me as part of our family picture.

So then what is a father? What is a Superhero? Clearly, it is not The Incredible Hulk. Michael wanted to be my Superhero, but somewhere between the waiting room and the delivery room at Evanston Hospital, he fell short.

Please do not misunderstand; it was never Michael's intention to disappoint me. The disappointment did not come right away; our life as a family started out all right. When he married my mother, an upper class, well-educated, white woman, he knew that they would face racial struggles. The relationship was not easy for their families and the rest of the world. My mom tells me their relationship was like the old Katharine Hepburn and Sidney Poitier movie; *Guess Who's Coming to Dinner?* Yet, through all the discrimination, Michael loved my mother and wanted to

raise a family with her. When he found out that I was coming into the world, he did his best to be my Superhero.

He learned how to play tennis by watching his Superhero, Arthur Ashe, the black tennis star. Michael wanted to teach me tennis so that I could grow up playing tennis with him. As a baby and a toddler he took me to see my black relatives from the South and told me stories about our family history. Even on the days when we were not playing with the tennis ball or talking to my grandmother Jane, he was still a Superhero, because he was there. Michael showed me he loved me by being an active part of my life and making me know that I was just as much a part of the black culture as I was the white culture…at least for the first three years of my life.

When I was three, my younger sister Stephanie was born. It was then that life began to change in our little Evanston town house. Michael seemed be around less and less. I did not realize it at first because I started preschool, but then there were nights when he did not come home and it was just mom, Stephanie, and me. Slowly tennis and time with Grandma Jane was filled with alcohol and drugs. My mother did not tell me at the time that Michael was involved in these things; rather he was, "at work." Yet, by the age of six, my mother ran out of patience and left my father.

We moved from our integrated neighborhood and school to the wealthy white suburbs of Denver to become the only black children in the community and in our new elementary school. My Superhero was gone, and I was left to find one on my own. Michael showed up periodically the rest of my life, mainly on Christmas and birthdays. Yet, it was never consistent, and for the past five years, it has become completely unpredictable if I will ever talk to or see him again.

I began to face the challenge of finding Superheroes at the end of high school and throughout college. I read Maya Angelou books on my own, took black studies film and literature courses in college, and visited black and integrated churches. I still did not have many black peers or role models in my life on a daily basis, but I have tried to find them when possible. Trying to feel comfortable in the black culture and looking for positive black role models for myself has become a pursuit of mine during my journey of adolescence and adulthood. This pursuit is not just for my own benefit, but also for my profession.

I am 21-years-old, living on my own for the first time, trying to make sense of what it means to be biracial and without a father. I look at the nine-year-old black students that I teach in the city of Chicago. Some of them come from broken homes and I think to myself, "They deserve a Superhero, too." Maybe it is my job to help them find one. And how will I do that? Through books, cultural events, people in our community, and with the children's family and friends, I will try to provide them with support and examples of role models and the richness of the black culture. But most of all, I will show them a Superhero by loving them. I will be in the classroom with them every day of the year and show them that I care about them. I cannot promise to be a Superhero to all of these children, but what I can do is be there for them, and show them that I love them.

When I lost Michael as my Superhero, I did not just lose my father. I also lost my main connection to my culture and feelings of self-worth in being both Black and White. I am not angry with Michael anymore, well, most of the time. Mostly, I am just sad—sad that he lost his ambition to be my Superhero. Demonstrating his love for me by being a healthy and active part of my life was the best way he could have been my Superhero.

Erasing the Past Pain with a Smile

- Nesheba Kittling

I have always loved the scratchy feel of a mustache and beard. Sometimes I walk along and a smile escapes as I recall the bristles against my skin. It took me a long time to remember why.

He used to come once, twice a year. I felt special. I felt special when the birthday checks and cards came for me, and when he took us shopping and let us buy the pretty lace dresses, matching socks, and patent leather shoes. I felt special until something inside me changed, that something that missed him and was no longer satisfied with the dresses and patent leather shoes.

I was so young I didn't know how to voice it. So, I would line my shoes up on the stairs during his trips. As he approached, I would throw them wildly at him, one by one. I started telling him and everyone else that he was not my father; my real father lived in New Mexico. I called him an imposter. I was four.

I stopped talking to him completely when I was 11. I referred to him by his first name. He did not refer to me at all. I hated him with a passion that only love could kill, and he didn't know how to love me. He wasn't able to be patient enough to bring me back to him. So, my life went on without my father.

High school graduation and then college came. I never looked in the audience for his face. I devised plans for my future that he never knew. I had trips to the emergency room where he never came to hold my hand. I was so sick and dehydrated that I was delusional, and he didn't take care of me. I found success.

I was given love and he missed it all. He has missed knowing me and that means he's missed out on everything I would have added to his existence.

He is a stranger, though that doesn't mean he hasn't added anything to my life. His absence taught me how to appreciate others' presence, and his inability to be there for me has made me stronger. In that way, I guess my father gave me love the only way he knew how—the hard way. So now, when I feel the scratch of a mustache on my face, I remember why and I don't cry. I smile.

To Compare My Love to My Mother's

- Gabrielle Lee

I'm not scared of you the way mom is because we love you differently.
She's come to depend on you.
I've only learned how to depend on myself.
Where was that male guidance you were supposed to contribute to my
adolescence?

"You know where I'm at if you ever need anything."

The only male guidance I've received is in between the sheets from men
whom I didn't love or even cared to communicate. They turned the lights
off.
You were supposed to be the first person of the opposite sex to whom I
gave my heart.
Instead I held their hands and barely saw yours doing anything more
than pulling back to hit my mother.
Huge amounts of alcohol consumed at the bar.

"It's not what you do, but how you do it."

While at home our stomachs are clenching and unclenching trying to
recall a meal without pancakes and second-hand smoke.
Boys and girls who belonged to easy girlfriends bragged about the Christmas and birthday gifts they'd received in our place.

"Don't get pregnant."

I was suspended from school for defending myself against your injustice.
Congratulations you have successfully donated to my DNA make-up;
our similar features include eye color, hair texture, and the form of our
hands.

Family photos, awards, and report cards go unnoticed by
you, because drugs turned you into "our father the invisible man."
No problem has been too tough for you to run away from.
Constantly leaving someone else, a more capable adult, to pick up the
pieces you broke.

"Read the syllabus."

Possibly the problem was that I didn't come with a get rich quick guide,
and you weren't ready to make a lifetime investment.
There's no chance for interest now. I don't need a father figure, and don't
want a man.
I'm scared I might like you, or that you might reject me again or make
me depend on you the way mom does.

"Don't make the same mistake twice."

Men are a mystery to me, and I don't have the time to find all the clues,
nor do I enjoy doing it.
I'm not scared of you the way mom is because we love you differently.

Missing in Action

- Sandra Morris

He that volleyed seed so willingly
Is gone,
Leaving woman and child to cry out
In anguish,
To deal with the pain of his loss alone.

A mother queries,
What Enemy has stolen him
Like a thief in the night
From their tent of love
Suddenly camouflaged by hate.

Was it the lure of furlough in new lands,
Or a lust for conquering unknown territory,
Or escape from the shackles of commitment,
Or differing charted paths through the jungle of life wrought.

By growth
By sudden clarity
By comeliness now grown stale?

Casualties bloodied
With gangrene wounds oozing
Confusion and pain on the inside
watch wraithlike specters of their fathers
disappear
over
the
hill.

Blurred Images

- Toya Lay

I had butterflies in my stomach. I did not want to visit my father today. Why even bother? I was officially a statistic. I told my mother this every time she brought up my father. He had been gone for eight years. He left without as much as a phone call. And for that I would be bitter forever. I just knew it...back then, anyway. I am sorry; guess I should start at the beginning, or at least, the beginning from where I can remember it; from where I can remember him....

Now let's see, 1977 was the year I was born. Guess you'd think my little ass wouldn't remember my early years. That is the funny thing, children do. I did. I have blurred images of sitting in the front row at church, listening to my father preach. After church, we'd go over to my aunt's house and have Sunday dinner. Family time. I always sat next to my father. I just had it like that even before my mother. I was daddy's baby. His Suga. And the whole family knew it. There was nothing he would deny my spoiled ass. I didn't understand the word "no." So when other people tried to say it to me I'd have violent tantrums. My father would peer over at me from under his glasses, and I'd immediately quiet down.

I remember putting on his after-shave when he went to work even though now, Stetson doesn't do shit for me. He was my idol, my provider, and my daddy who in my eyes, could do no wrong even when my grandmother called him a "no good nigga," and even when he introduced me to his "lady friend." One day, my mother sat me down to say my father was leaving, but I could see him whenever I wanted.

When I was five, he came to pick me up for one of our weekend visits. Yolanda, the lady friend, a.k.a my stepmother, was waiting in the car seven months pregnant. I guess the whole scene was strange to my mother since Yolanda NEVER came within five feet of our house, and the packed bags in the car didn't help either.

You ever seen your great-grandmother chase after a car? Well I did that day. Maybe the funny look on my mother's face when the car door closed set her off, or maybe it was my grandmother shouting obscenities at the back of my father's head as he wrapped the seatbelt around me. Regardless, they blocked the car at a stop sign with their bodies, my grandmother wielding a broom, my great-grandmother, a wrench, and my mother on the porch screaming. And what was I doing? Crying uncontrollably. I knew my father wanted to take me with him to Ohio where he'd bought a new house to go along with his new job, new church, and new life.

I had remained silent, even at five-years-old, because I couldn't let my daddy leave me. But he did. He never called to say good-bye after I was pulled from the car and he sped off with a broken windshield. He never called to say he made it. I learned of step-brothers through pictures and long letters from cousins, but never him. I learned about his short trips back to Chicago from aunts and uncles, but never him. I learned his job was moving him back to Chicago from a letter he wrote after eight years of confusion, heartache, and resentment.

I was 16. I was bitter. I was jealous. I was a statistic. I would muster up the courage though, to drive over my aunt's for a Sunday dinner. My hair was freshly done. My nails were immaculate and my clothes were all brand new. I should've left the tags on them. I wanted my father to see me as a woman now.

I wanted him to know he missed eight years of my life. I almost wished he'd have trouble recognizing me. Would he feel bad though? Would I see even the slightest expression of guilt? I would soon find out. Who did this mutha fucker think he was anyway? My father? No! He was just a man now. Reduced to shit in my eyes now. Just another nigga I was going to impress, give a phony smile to, and then leave wondering what I really thought of him.

However, when I got there, my anger just melted. He recognized me in a room full of cousins. I was daddy's Suga again. My aunt had saved a chair for me next to him at the table. He talked to me non-stop the whole time. He apologized and tried to explain all those years. Those smoked filled years...those suicidal years...those unhappy years.

The next eight years went by quick. I had written a letter to my father the day I graduated from high school, expressing the anger and love I felt for him. He responded with a letter that wasn't full of apologies, yet he stated how much he loved me, and I had every right to be angry. Was I still bitter? Yes. But with lots of prayer and time my heart has healed. I now know my father as the imperfect but beautiful individual that he is. I still consider myself a statistic, but with a happier ending than most.

Unresolved

- Pam Osbey

i'm hoping against hope
that we will resolve these issues
I want to know why
you don't talk to me
and why you pushed me away
and why you've never said
"i'm sorry about emotionally
abusing you"

but maybe you have no words to say
I must give this negativity away
lay it into the dust
and bury it with you
since you are laying like
you're dead

I just don't understand
why you'd disregard
your own flesh and blood
like it's never been created

i'm still here
and I know you're still
breathing

so dad, why are you
still ignoring me
and my brothers

this I will never understand
and yes, I hurt
but I understand that
God has a bigger plan for me
and I must use my energy for
good and not evil

and even though this issue
is unresolved
and you've aborted your
children
I know that all men are not dogs
and that all men aren't irresponsible
about handling their business as parents
to their kids...
I just know that you're
my father
and i'm still your seed
and I do forgive you
and i'm okay

i'm okay
whether or not
you are in my life

but I hope you understand
your silence and your total
ignorance has not made me
stopped me from being
the beautiful sistah
the beautiful spirit
that God created

and I forgive you
I understand that's the way
you're built

I just hope you can sleep
at night
knowing you threw away
precious time with your
children

it's resolved in my mind
that i've done all I can do
and i'm closing the book
on this part of my life
with you

Daddy's Little Girl

- Kieshawn Middleton

I am my number one enemy because I am you.

I was two going on 35, passing up those essential childhood years, trading them in for womanhood...so soon, too soon. A two-year-old "woman" left to be a mother to my mother. You were the cause of the tears of a strong and independent woman, yet it was up to me to dry them. I was the one to mend my mother's broken heart and endure the frustration that bore your name. And my reward? A blonde-haired, blue-eyed Barbie doll that resembled your new girlfriend, or sporadic visits, which I accepted with gratitude because you convinced me that they were tokens of your love. I later realized that your "tokens of love" were lies, just another way out.

You escaped your responsibilities and left them for me to carry because they were too heavy for you, and I smiled to hide the pain of carrying two crosses instead of one. I couldn't let anyone see me cry. And now that I've finally reached the age of adulthood, I cannot look into my love's eyes because my eyes are yours. I have inherited your poisonous touch, but I will continue to love you. I promise that you will never hear your future grandbabies speak your name spitefully or look at you in disgust. This I promise because you are me and I am you.

I am daddy's little girl.

Fruit of Corrupt Seed

- Johannas Williams

I am Johannas.
Daughter to an amazing woman
Who did nothing
but worked and loved hard
Her entire life.
Sister to hurt women
The three of us ambitious, beautiful...
just alike.
And my brothers...
Far too much of men for me
To ever put into mere words.
But I never understood why it is
My father left his family
And every explanation of it
Was either a lie or completely absurd.
What kind of man abandons
His wife and kids
In a strange land?
Where I never heard
of traffic or sirens.
Left with the evil grandmother
That treated her grandchildren
Like heathens and tyrants.
One Sunday morning, I woke up
To the sounds of my mother screaming
And losing her mind.
My grandmother lying on the floor,
Medics rushing up the stairs
As if they were competing with the
Speed of light or time.
Stroke, heart attack, or cardiac arrest...
No one ever knew the real cause,
The curiosity was left alone...

Or better yet...put to rest.
I knew the truth.
The truth is that she was tired.
Tired of losing herself
And leaving her own identity
To the memory of her family.
The truth is that she was dying.
Dying from a withering mind
That lost the ability
To remember persons, places, and time.
The truth is that she was angry.
Angry at her children
Who put occupation and love life
Over her own.

Angry that her daughter
Would escape to various places around the globe
But had to force herself to come home.
Angry that her sons,
Whom she thought she raised to be real men...
Wanted nothing to do with her,
Invisibly held up signs
That read, "Refer to the hand."
My father never once told me anything
About his real father
Or the side of his family thereof.
Just leniently left it in the dark
And claimed to be sparing our sanity
In the name of love.
Daddy, did you really love me?
Did you really love me when you
Chose to work in Virginia
And not in the same dwelling as your seeds?
Did you love me when the only
Sign of your existence
Was in the form of a check
In my time of emotional need?
Did you really love me,
When you sent me fifty dollars
For my 18th birth date?

MY SOUL TO HIS SPIRIT

Or was that a selfish act
Of self-forgiveness for yourself
You sent in hopes to compensate?
Nothing can compensate
For almost ten years of my life
That you consciously made yourself stray.
Ten years, developing as a woman
Through my mother and
Never learning my father's way.
Ten years forced to grow up
in the name of society's
statistic-painful- something's...
That said
the majority of black girls raised
In a single parent home
Is and always will be nothing.
I'm eighteen-years-old
And I still wet the bed,
Only this time with sweat.
Demons and fallen angels
Attacking my soul, making threats
in the midst of my silent rest.
Stomach churning-skin burning mornings
Waking up with scars on my thighs
And deep bruises on my breasts.

A wise teacher once told me
That the demons represented
Every man that lustfully laid hands and eyes on me.
Coming back to warn me
To stop leaving increments of my soul
On their beds,
Along with my identity.
I listened very carefully
And applied his words to my life.
And sure enough,
I went back to the very same men
And the demons came back at night.
Voices in my head.
Johannas keep your legs closed.

I should have stayed in my clothes.
Maybe there was a possibility
That my bronze skin wouldn't have manipulated
Already horny and stimulated minds,
Hungry fingers, and eyes...
My flesh was the only part of me that smiled
All the while,
My soul cried...parts of me died
While I lied bare,
Feeling my hymen tear.
Lord, I needed you there
When the beginning of my downfall occurred.
Dreams deferred
As I began to believe I was a grown woman
That saw all there was to see
Heard all there was to be heard.
I felt like a bird,
Compelled to swoop down
And scoop up every fish in the sea.
Taking advantage of the physical offering
To quiet my yearning plea.
All the while hell is screaming,
Pleading, and bleeding for me.
Like a foolish jezebel,
I proceeded to spread my knees
Welcoming in all foreign and local enemies
To put on a raincoat,
take a number,
and have a seat.
Easy defeat
On the territory of no one else, but me.
2:33
One Friday morning
I finally saw the light.
Not through the beams of the sunlight
Through my blinds...

But within
The deep reflection of myself
In the streams of my mind.

MY SOUL TO HIS SPIRIT

Suddenly I was free,
Happy, not yearning, and more refined.
I crossed paths with the answer
On my own,
And it was far from anything
I had to seek to find.
It already existed
In my life all that time.
All that time I felt the need
To define myself through
The love or lust of a man...
All that time I spent—wasted
Running after truth and patience.
And the answer was right here
In my very own hands.
I became
True
to
Myself.

Dinner at My Father's House, December 2000

- Opal Palmer Adisa

I was in New York on business, so I took the opportunity to call my father with the intention of visiting him. As I hoped, he was happy to hear from me and invited me to dinner. I accepted eagerly, determined once and for all to ask him why he had not contacted me for ten years, from when I was ten-years-old to 20. I wanted to have a heart-to-heart, come-clean-once-and-for-all talk with my father. I realized that those years were still splattered with pain and it was way past time to heal my feelings of abandonment and truly forgive the past.

I arrived at my father's suburban home an hour later than I said, as my ride was delayed. We embraced, tentatively, and my father invited my friend and me into the living room, and then almost immediately brought us drinks and cookies. Although my friend was only dropping me off, he accepted, and we sat around, drinking and engaging in small talk. I observed my father keenly as if seeing him for the first time. He was a well-preserved man, short, elegant yet simple. I noticed that there was orderliness about him and that he carried himself with decorum, as if he knew he was important. I smiled thinking about my own haughtiness, which I had always assumed I got from my mother. Although my father has lost sight in one eye to glaucoma, he moved purposefully like a man who is about doing things. He had aged well, hardly any gray, only a few wrinkles, but I realized that he was much smaller than the image of him that is indelible in my head from a child. Anxious for answers, I scanned the living room that hadn't changed much since my first visit the summer of 1975. There was still plastic on the sofa. For whom was he preserving this furniture?

After an acceptable time, politeness aside, my friend begged off with another appointment. Once he left, my father seated me around the dining table that was already set and announced that dinner had been waiting. He declined my offer to help, insisted that I sit and relax as he stacked three albums on the record player before he began putting the various dishes on the table, an enormous spread, which he prepared himself. Old ballads, that I hadn't heard since I was a child, issued from the record player. I asked him about the title of some of the cuts as he walked to and from the kitchen with food and juice, the lyrics springing forth from the recess of my memory.

Over a delicious meal of baked turkey, rice, salad, and steamed carrots and pumpkin, we small talked. I asked about Patsy, this sister who still doesn't feel like a sister, and whose whereabouts always seemed a mystery. I inquired about cousins, his nieces, with whom I was close before the family splintered, moving to the USA. I collected details about their marriages, children and grandchildren, and got their recent addresses. As my father cleared the table and washed dishes, again declining my offer to help, I marveled over his record collection. No CD in this batch. Nothing more recent than the early 80s. Time seemed frozen here, and I wondered if this was an indication of his memory.

After my father was through with the kitchen, I invited him to join me at the table so we could talk. With sweaty underarms, I couldn't help but feel like a little girl petitioning her father for some favor. I turned over the rehearsed phrases in my head, but the words came out direct.

"Why didn't you contact us for ten years?" I asked, looking at him keenly.

"There was never a moment or a day that I didn't love and think about you and Dawn," he began almost immediately as if he had been waiting to tell me this.

"But you never wrote. Never sent us birthday cards or anything," I rejoined on the heels of his words.

He appeared to reflect on my accusations. I hated how I was feeling, like the little girl wanting her father, but I knew I had to be done with this part of my life, this need to have the past filled in—a puzzle with missing pieces. I still wanted and desperately needed to hear him offer some kind of explanation.

"When I first came to America, I wasn't straight, wasn't legal. Things weren't easy for a long time...."

I knew that story well, unrecorded as it was. It is the stories of countless people from the West Indies who lost children, wives, husbands, parents, and each other in the process of getting a green card. I hadn't imagined my father, educated, a chemist, respected back home in Jamaica, as one of many immigrants trying to find a footing. I listened closely as he related his story, but after a while it didn't matter any more. In that moment, hearing his explanation, I chided myself about why I had made such a big deal about those lost years for so long. But the truth was, I needed to hear him say it, I had to have my father admit, confess that he loved me even though he never contacted me for all those years.

After he was through with his explanation, my father invited me upstairs to his study. As I entered, I was confronted with several pictures of myself in various stages and at different ages. Pictures of my sister and me and our children filled all the walls, along with a copy of some writing award I received. The maxim, "Action speaks louder than words," had weight that evening because in that moment, if I ever doubted that my father loved me, seeing images of myself on his wall, in his private and cherished space, dispelled all doubts. And although our conversation felt like two long lost friends meeting up again, somewhat unsure about how personal to get with each other, I was happy and relieved. I had found my way back to my father; I was not a forsaken little girl anymore.

We poured through his photo albums, and he pointed out relatives whose names I had forgotten or perhaps had never known. I saw pictures of my father as a young man that I didn't ever remember seeing, and I certainly didn't remember ever knowing that he was a sprinter in high school. At my request, he graciously loaned me some of the pictures to copy for my own album, especially those of my deceased grandfather and grandmother when they were young, and a few pictures of my sister and me when we were five and three-years-old, respectively.

When I left close to 10:00 p.m. that night, well after my father's normal 8:30 p.m. bedtime, I knew I had finally shed the past and it could no longer keep me in bondage. "Good night daddy," I said as I embraced him goodbye. I felt light, and was happy that I was my father's daughter. That night just before I went to bed, for the first time that I could remember as an adult, I gave thanks for my father connecting with my mother to make me. I vowed, no matter what, to always be in contact with him, not out of any sense of obligation, but because I wanted us to be in each other's life.

They had a short visit, but he showed them his garden, the pumpkins and tomatoes he grew and the well-tended yard. In the warm afternoon of August, they sat outside, sipping juice, eating biscuits, and talking. They brought their camera and eagerly took lots of pictures, which they now cherish. Like me, my children were impressed with their grandfather's study, walls of photographs, some of themselves, some of me they had never seen. They too came to realize that even though they did not see or talk to their grandfather, that they meant something to him. He even showed them some of the cards and notes they had sent him over the years. My son was duly impressed and told me we needed to visit grandpa more often. I assured him that we would.

When we left my father's house after a satisfying visit, I felt as if I had fulfilled two important promises. The first to my youngest child, taking her to meet her grandfather, my father; and the second, to myself and my father—at last, I had allowed the ebb of the sea to wash the debris of the past into the belly of the ocean.

My father and I live on opposite coasts, too far to visit often and try to bridge those gaps—so much about me he doesn't know and never will, and vice versa. However, we are living in the present, certain of each other's love. All my nagging questions have disappeared, replaced with a quiet appreciation of how fortunate I am to have both parents alive and to be in touch with both. Orlando is my father and I am happy we reconciled the past. I call him daddy, although it feels new coming from my mouth. I respect and honor his desire for me to address him as daddy.

I vow to share as much of my life with my father as he is willing to share, and to tell my children all the stories I remember of him. I am delighted that my children now know their grandfather and have a real person to go with the pictures. They write and call him, and daily learn more about their long-denied maternal grandfather.

I am enormously glad that time has been so kind to my father and me, and daily I offer blessings to the universe for reuniting us, forever father and daughter.

Non-Existent

COULD PASS ME ON THE STREET

"I never knew you, but I wish I
had. Maybe my experiences with
boys wouldn't have been so bad."

"... we passed each other on a crowded train."

"I no longer wish to
thank him for being apart
of my creation."

CHAPTER IV

Non-Existent: COULD PASS ME ON THE STREET

We all have a father, but do we all know our fathers? Daughters of loving fathers can answer this question with an emphatic "yes." Daughters of distant fathers can also answer this question in the affirmative and daughters of abandoned fathers had the luxury, if only for a season, to know their fathers as well. However, daughters of non-existent fathers come into this world with nothing more than his name and a Griot history of who he is from others. For reasons known and unknown, these women will never have a cultivated relationship with their fathers and are often left wondering "why?" The psychological impact can lead to what Reverend Fox calls the "Three D's: depression, despondence, and despair." Her advice is to seek out male mentors, surrogate fathers, whom black women, can trust and can receive wise counsel.

His failure to be there from the beginning and throughout her life leaves a void that she yearns to be fulfilled. The sentiments of these stories range from times when she thought she recognized his face in a crowd and the rush of emotions that she felt in that moment, to the rage she experiences every time she is reminded of him. Her stories are written to an intangible recipient whom she may never meet; therefore, she addresses her sentiments to that space in her life that was created the day she realized that daddy doesn't exist for her.

Letters to Daddy

- Samaiya Ewing

Dear Father:

I don't know who you are. I only know that you were gone before I was born, out of my life, out of my mother's. I sometimes think of you, not fondly I'm afraid, but I do wonder if you would still have left if you truly understood what you were abandoning us for. I remember when I first found out your name, at age 12, your existence made a liar of my mother, whom I already knew to be less than perfect, but loved nonetheless. I would lie awake at night, dreaming you were a rich tycoon of one sort or another, and that you'd come to sweep me away to a better place, a happier place. Even now, I sometimes think of you as being filthy rich, except I've no need of your rescue. Be warned wherever you are, that if you are rich, you'd best hide your fortune well. For if we chance to meet, I will not hesitate to take you for all you're worth, and more. I am not angry with you, not really. I understand why you did what you did. I too start things that I've no hope of finishing, I suppose that is my gift from you.

Yours in Fickleness,

Samaiya

Dear Stepfather #1:

I know no more about you than I do my real father. I do feel though, that your sin is greater than his. It is one thing to run from a fetus, the unknown, but quite another to abandon a human being, a girl, a child, with hopes, dreams, and feelings of her own.

I remember using my pink jump rope to tie you to a chair, hoping to keep you with me for just a bit longer, but this was ineffective. It is my humble suggestion that in the future you refrain from spending five years with something before deciding to give up on it. Do not waste its time, don't waste your own. Perhaps you and my real father could have coffee sometime, and discuss the most humane way to abandon a child. He has mastered the concept. You dear daddy, have a lot of catching up to do.

In Hopes of Self Improvement,

Samaiya

Dear Stepfather #2:

I would say I hate you, but then you'd win. I would say I love you, but I'd be lying. I hate you. You win. I hate what you did to me, to my mother. I used to pray for you to die, and when year after year passed and you lived, I gave up on God. I remember when you first came to us, tall and foreboding. I knew there was trouble ahead, but when my mother asked me, age six, if I minded if she married you, I said "no." Even then her happiness was more important to me than to you.

I was right to be suspicious, crack turned out to be your only true love. I watched you beat my mother. I watched you beat my sisters. I watched you beat me. I woke up on random mornings to find your drug paraphernalia strewn across my bathroom sink. You had your own. I walked in fear of you until the day I realized that you were afraid of me. I listened to you call my mother names like "bitch," and "whore." I watched you push her around, my little sister trapped inside her belly. And when they came, three girls, one after the other, I took care of them because she couldn't and you wouldn't. I pity you. I pity you, because you never knew what you had, blinded as you were by the desire for things that could never be yours. I hate you because now when I tell people that I'm a lesbian, they ask if you abused me, and all I can do is stare at them tongue tied, confused, wondering why my sexuality must always be linked to your stupidity.

I hate you because you were never brave enough to be open about your hatred for me, instead pretending to love me, though you and I both knew that you loved your real children, not the sullen bastard child forced upon you. They knew as well, even now when they see how you treat their mother; they condemn me and not you.

It is my fault that you left; my fault that they no longer live with you; my fault that you and my mother do not get along; and my fault that you are who you are. If only I had been a better daughter, if only I had suffered in silence, if only I had turned the other way, we would all still be a family. The American Dream, passive-aggressive suicide with a smile.

God was a tease in those days. I remember my mother fought back once, stabbed you with a kitchen knife. I was in the basement, watching your body being loaded onto a stretcher, blood dripping onto our front porch, and I jumped for joy, sure that you were dead. Raggedy Ann and I had a celebratory tea party/funeral only to discover later, that she had missed a major artery by an inch. I prayed to God to give my mother better aim. Yet when my chance came, I too, allowed you to live. I watched you gasping for breath on your bedroom floor, wheezing, "Call the ambulance Samaiya." I told myself that if you weren't dead in half an hour that I'd have to get help.

I almost didn't. I left you there on the brink of death, while I finished my math homework. I was 13.

At 14, I discovered Karma, and my new mantra for life became, "He'll die before I will; he'll die before I will." I was convinced that the universe would punish you for your indiscretions. Unfortunately, I was not patient then, nor am I now. So began my sabotage. I found your social security number and called phone sex lines masquerading as you, and waited for the bill to come. It came, two hundred dollars complete with an explosion from my mother. She kicked you out, I rejoiced. I put rubbing alcohol in the peroxide, hid it in my room, and waited. I filled a sandwich bag with a suspicious white substance (cornstarch), and left it in my mother's nightstand drawer.

I found your real supply of cocaine, and gave it to a friend at school, no charge. I tried (in vain) to ruin your life as I felt you had ruined mine. I had forgotten life's most important lesson. "The best revenge is living well." I have scars from my time with you, wounds that will never heal. I find myself in relationships that are disturbingly similar to my relationships with you, relationships in which I must constantly defend myself, mentally, physically, emotionally, and verbally. I am emotionally unavailable, not just to others, but also to myself. And so when I say that I hate you, perhaps it is really that I hate the pieces of myself that came from you. I don't believe in God, yet, on occasion, I still pray for you to die.

Samaiya

Lost but Never Found

- Mae Koen

I met my father for the first time 10 years ago....

For a long time, I knew where my father worked, but I was afraid to seek him out. A friend of my mother kept up with his family and knew how to contact him. Under the encouragement of a friend, I decided to seek him out. Why I never did before? I suppose I was afraid. I didn't want anything from him; I just wanted to place a face on the title of father. I didn't even want to develop a relationship with him; I just wanted to know who he was.

I wondered for years what happened that he never came around. I was in several failed relationships, and one time, my mother brought it to my attention that I was looking for a father figure in the men I chose.

My mother would never say too much about my father. I never knew what happened between the two of them, but I know whatever it was it caused her not to like me very much. When I was old enough to understand my mother's closest sister told me something that changed my life. She told me that my father raped my mother. It made sense to me then why my mother seemed to hate me at times. I was old enough to understand even though the pain of the past could never be erased. My mother didn't talk to my aunt for several years after that. I tried to get her to talk to me about it, but she avoided it for a long time.

I told her she at least owed me that much, seeing that I wanted to know. Finally, she explained to me what happened. She was 14 and he was 17. She thought he was cute, but he took advantage of a young, naive, curious girl. She said she didn't even know she was pregnant until her mother (my grandmother) noticed.

She sent my mother to Detroit to have me. I also found out that in addition to my mother, he (my father) impregnated two other girls in high school. Those pregnancies resulted in one boy, and two other girls. One girl he impregnated twice.

When I sought him out, we decided to meet in a public place. I knew immediately that he was my father or the "sperm donor," because I look more like him than my mother. I also found out that his other son,

Michael, also sought him out and hit him when he met him. I wanted to hit him too. I felt he was a big reason that my mother is so unhappy and that we don't have a healthy relationship.

I got an opportunity to meet the other two girls, one in person and one on the phone. Ironically, their mother also treated them horribly when they were children. I wonder if he really knew the chain reaction that he caused, getting young girls pregnant, and in my mother's case, doing it by force. I never got an opportunity to meet the brother, I only know his name is Michael.

A couple of months after I met my father I ran into him in a parking lot of a grocery store. I sarcastically said "hello father." My son who was ten at the time looked at him with disbelief and said to him, "Are you my mother's father?" and he had the nerve to say, "That's what they tell me," although I look like he spit me out. If I had the courage I would've hit him right then and there. Meeting him was a disappointment, but I did accomplish my goal of placing a face on the title. Maybe deep down inside I did want him to be someone I could get to know and develop a relationship with, but instead he turned out to be an asshole.

I ran into him one other time after that. We passed each other on a crowded train. I was getting on and he was getting off. I recognized him and he didn't even know who I was. What a strange feeling that was, to see your own father who brought you into this world and he not even know who you are. Then I thought, had I not sought him out we would've passed each other and never even knew. I carry that feeling of emptiness and disappointment with me to this day.

QuesEr:
Questions Eagerly Raised

- Tawyeh Nishan-Do

The cool desert sand of QuesER rushed frantically between my toes. I dug them way down deep inside it, because I knew that it wasn't time. But it was time and I knew they would be coming for me soon. Further away I could hear sounds of string music being played against the wailing of other child souls. I wonder if they felt the same way I did. They also did not want to go.

Elder spirits would form tight circles around each child that holds their ancestral goals. Their long ears drape the ground as they listen to each Earth Mother make their wishes, and then they whisper into the children's underdeveloped ears. They tell each child what is expected of them and then they send them on their way. There are no directions given on how to get there. We were to travel by the voices of our Earth Mother. This was the Elders' way of breaking us into the Earth's rhythm.

I almost lost my way by the voice of my Earth Mother. She was screaming the whole way as my soul was trying to reach the body of her fetus. I didn't understand why my course was such an unaccepted ride until I was delivered and born eight years from the Sun and I was light years from QuesER.

I figured myself old enough to ask her why I didn't look like the man she married, and she knew that I knew. She told me that while she waited for me to be born she wished that I had dreamy eyes.

This explained why I grew up knowing that there was something wrong with my existence. My eyes saw it when I was on QuesER, and the Elder spirits knew that I knew but it was time and they had to send me.

Twenty-five years born from the Sun and light years from QuesER, I have developed senses that have in ways made my time here incomplete. However the goal still remains and I still have my eyes. I use them to search the Elder Spirits' faces on QuesER. Hoping one day that I can recognize his face and feel his essence amongst the many themes of my dreams.

Dead, Missing, or Alive?

- Kimberly Cole

Dead?
If that's the way it is
I'll admit, it tickles me
Dead almost like dad
Except inserted an e
Representing elusive,
Endangered and empty
Or opposite ends of an extreme
Always been—never be

Ma said your name was Fred
Which I believe to be true
Funny how it rhymes with dead
And the only part of you I knew

Missing?
The only possibility
With potential to move me
It's what you were or are
That's certainly not the mystery
And it's not that I miss you
But what you've missed unknowingly
My smile, my charisma,
My intellectual abilities

So, my heart is slightly open
Deep down, I'm quietly hoping
You're sick, unconscious, and missing
But didn't or wouldn't choose to be

Alive?
Well, how unnecessary
What could you be worth, at the age of thirty?
See, all that could have been lost
By a little girl not having a daddy
Was made up with ease
By other members of the family
And what was left to do
Mama did, unselfishly

So this will take some time
A tribute to those who've fulfilled every need
A way to help you understand
How others nurtured the growth of your seed

A **big brother** to spoil me
A t**win brother** to play
Oh yeah, you missed out on two lives
Made the same day
Older **cousins** for protection
My **brothers' friends** for that too
With a team like this
How could I lose?

Uncle Leon, now gone
But still alive in my heart and mind
Yielded to every promise
A party, computer, and school supplies
Uncle Bruce, gone too and not blood related
Always showed up on time
Whether it was shoes, clothes or favorite foods
His character was sublime

To **Uncle Joe**, his favorite niece
Alive and present still today
Makes me feel special
In a "daddy's girl" kind of way
To **Uncle Adlai**, a complete beauty
To **Cousin Slick**, like one of his own
With all of them around me
I've been a princess; ready for a Queen's thrown

And just to "keep it real"
My **mother** was really **mom** and dad
And worked twice as hard
For all to be had
She dished out the discipline
And maintained the house too
Never spoke a bad word
About you or what you didn't do

Now my final thought
To hold close and to keep
I have a **husband** to complete me
And give me more than I can dream
So if you are alive
What could you do or be?
Maybe good for your sake
But nothing in that for me

Dead?
I'll accept,
Most readily
No need for more questions,
And even a birth to peace

Missing?
Not likely,
But probable
I'm open to its disguise
A safe place for you to stay, if you're wise

Alive?
I'll simply refuse
And even stronger reject
Avoiding the chance to confuse
Or deal with your neglect

So this is all the time I'll give you
At least I can say I tried
From my soul to your spirit
Dead, Missing, or Alive!

I Never Knew Lawrence

- Michele Matthews

Daddy
I never knew you but I wish I had
To be able to look into your eyes and call you "Dad"
Now you're gone and I'll never have the chance
To get the details of yours and mama's romance
Ya'll were never married
In fact you belonged to another
Sneaking and creeping
All just to see my mother
Was she just a booty call?
Or did you really care?
I was the product
So I believe these questions are fair

Damn Daddy
I never knew you but I wish I had
To be able to call you on the phone and say, "Hey Dad!"
I didn't even know you existed until the age of 16
My stepfather was the King and Mama the Queen
Then you became the guy who planted the seed
Just my biological—besides you had other kids to feed
Then at 19 more questions arose
Did I inherit his walk, his talk, his eyes, his nose?
Who am I and Who was he?
Mama set up a meeting
So for myself I could see
When you first saw me your eyes filled with tears
What had you been thinking for the past 19 years?

MY SOUL TO HIS SPIRIT

Damn Daddy
I never knew you but I wish I had
Maybe my experiences with the boys wouldn't have been so bad
I would have felt much better about me
And not felt so much shame
I would have believed in love
And not treated it as a game
Now the man I'm with is married to another
Sneaking and creeping
Just like so many others

Daddy
I never knew you but I wish I had
To be able to look into your eyes and call you "Dad"

Foreign

- Regina Jennings

I struggle to see you
Fix you in my head and heart
Only memory flakes replace a ghost
Invisible, like an ancestor

I recall when I was young and you bent
Down like a tree branch you bent
To tell me an identity already nailed in me
You said, do you know what I am to you
Despite my mother denying you fatherhood
Up and down I shook my head
And you said, I am your father

I pillow fluffed when you echoed father
Although unsure whether a mirage
or miracle
You remained Buster in my mouth
and father
Floating around a fantasy

You never lived in my grandmother's house
Where Chips barked in the yard and guests
Used the wooden bathroom outside

In my mother's later house your absence
In the asylum where I sniffed hell in a woman's eye
You sent me strange cards in my mother's house
From prison
I got a card I guess a few days a year
All an identical cryptographic message:

"Someone's thinking of you
in a special sort of way

and send this card to say
hello and tell you so today"

Where is your grave your geography
Were you ever a little boy, a teenager
Your favorite foods what were they
What made laughter laminate your face
You empty space

When I saw you on South Philadelphia streets
When I abandoned adolescence
You served drugs more than sobriety
and ragged
You ran from me
Pretending blindness I realized
and respected
The back of your legs, flying

Your brother Sweetning spoke the message:
Of death
Wiring my confusion a collage of absence
In funerary words. Why look for me
A silent bomb and tomb my life without

I went back to playing wall ball with Buck
The brother I married later and left

The flavor of father, Dad, pop, daddy
or mother, ma, mom, mommy
is it vanilla

I creamed too soon without parents
On my own lacerating racism
Fugitive status became my father
Until Panther milk nourished my people love

But, I still find men like distant countries
An exciting vacation that always disappears

Ice Cream vs. Stranger

- Nkiru Nso-Ani

A bit of a recluse. He was a recluse in high school." James, my aunt's boyfriend said. "I knew your father in high school."

"Mom, tell me about my father!" I asked one day. "He was a black Muslim. We dated for three years before I got pregnant with you. His name was James!"

All this information was given to me at different times over the course of my 24-year life. I asked several times if my father knew about me. To my shock, each time the answer was, "yes, your father knows you exist." My grandmother told me that she contacted him when she found out that my mother was pregnant with me. She asked him what he planned to do and to my shock once again he said he was going to take care of me, that he would be there.

I have only seen my father once. I was five-years-old. My mother had taken me to Baskin-Robbins to get some ice cream. I walk in with my mother and a friend, and I don't even notice the man in there, on the same side of the counter as I was. I assume that the man and my mother exchanged words and then she told me that he was my father. I looked at him in disbelief. I shook my head no, and he replied, "Yes, I am." He proceeded to ask me why I was so bad in school, and I lied, denying any wrong doings. I was a little worn out over the constant discussion about my misbehavior and here a stranger was questioning me. Since I was a "grown five-year-old," I wanted to ask a question.

"If you are my father, then what is your middle name?

"The same as yours," was the reply.

"Monique?" (Thinking it odd that a man's middle name would be Monique.)

He nodded yes. My mother said it was time for us to go and we left. I don't remember looking back, nor caring to continue with the stranger that I had just met in the ice cream shop.

As I approached my teens, I secretly longed for a relationship with my father. My thinking, however juvenile, was that my father should pay for my wedding since my mother raised me. Now since I am no longer legally allowed to be married in any state, I decided to waive that request that he pay for it or that he even have the privy to know that I am getting committed to someone.

Upon reaching "adulthood" the wish to have a relationship with my father has waned slightly. I am no longer curious to know what this man was/is like. I no longer wish to know which one of my features resembles his. I no longer wish to know how he was/is mentally in order to under-stand my depressive episodes, which I can most certainly attribute to him. I also no longer wish to thank him for my pretty feet that I know, without a doubt, came from him (years of observation of the feet on my maternal side). I no longer wish to thank him for being part of my creation. I no longer wish these things...I want them.

Amended

TIME AND FORGIVENESS
HEALS ALL WOUNDS

"Forgiveness is about releasing yourself from the hurt."

"...God knew that a part of my healing must include my father."

"Whether or not my father and I ever get back to our original place of love is unimportant."

CHAPTER V

Amended: TIME AND FORGIVENESS HEALS ALL WOUNDS

The only true prerequisite for forgetting is time. Time allows you to replace what you once remembered with something new and it is in time that everything and everyone changes. However, what time does not afford you is the compassion to erase past pain and hurt. Those emotions linger with time; therefore, time alone is never enough. The daughters in *Amended* have added forgiveness to time. They are choosing to forgive sporadic fathers, negligent fathers, and even non-existent fathers. At key points in their lives, they took the bandage of time off the wound his fatherly behavior left in their lives and healed it with forgiveness.

For many of the daughters, this universal, Christian principle was not immediate. Forgiveness took time and for others they continue to forgive "daddy" and themselves for internalizing the anger and judging all other men accordingly. They are finally at a place where they are willing to forgive. They teach all of us the most invaluable lesson with regards to repairing broken relationships...you must forgive yourself and the offender. These women have made a conscious choice to do more than forget their fathers' decisions in time, but to elevate their feelings to a permanent place of forgiveness with time. Regardless of the reason, they are releasing him from all paternal sins and accepting daddy for who he is.

Pimps Anonymous

- Tina Fakhrid-Deen

Sweet Charlie Brown is my daddy's nickname. Like Charlie Brown, he is kind, in search of himself, and afraid to commit. Unlike sorry Charlie, he is confident, handsome, and very intelligent. He owned several successful businesses with a high school education under his belt, prides himself on being a street-wise hustler, and is a true ladies man. As a father, he was gentle, nurturing, and responsible during my youth. He provided food, shelter, discipline, advice, and plenty of love to his baby girl. He willingly took the reins when my mother was incapable of caring for me. He was my father, my teddy bear, and my best friend. At age 11, I went to him at the sight of my first menstrual cycle and demanded that he show me what to do with a maxi pad. Like the man that he is, he stepped up to that challenge and every other that I threw at him from birth until my twelfth birthday, when womanhood began to set in and the contradictions became too fierce. For a young girl, he was everything that you could want in a "daddy."

The problem is my daddy is a pimp. He is a charismatic, fun, gentle, and witty pimp, but a pimp nonetheless. He is an insatiable womanizer who gets his money by all means necessary and puts Iceberg Slim to shame. He has married and divorced four times. More than ten women have lived in his home at one time or another (not including his mama and siblings) claiming to be his "woman." I would dare to say that he has had more women than the projects have roaches.

All of these women had to give up many of their valued assets: money, property, sex, freedom, and dignity to be with him, but they weren't the only ones who gave up their valuables. My father lost me, his only daughter, to his lifelong addiction to ass. And by default, I "gave up" all trust in men.

At age 12, I became one of Charlie's "women" and therefore, expendable. I became a woman with too much mouth and too much sense for my own good. I became hardheaded, slick, and "fast," like my father's other conquests. For the first time in my life, I fell into the "them" category, a mindless, emotional, stupid, "do anything for Charlie" woman. I couldn't talk to boys if I wanted to please Charlie. I couldn't stay outside after the streetlights came on if I didn't want to be accused of being a streetwalker. I couldn't back talk his women. I couldn't request training bras. I couldn't ask why his wife didn't get angry when his girlfriends called the house, and I definitely couldn't ask if my husband would turn out the same way. Questioning my father's actions became a constant battle, with me on the losing end. My knowing eyes became my father's worst enemy because they were the eyes to his soul, pleading him to be a better man, a challenge he wasn't willing to confront. And at age 12, my big mouth, my knowing eyes, and me got kicked out of Charlie Brown's house—for good.

I left on my twelfth birthday with emotional battle scars, determined to never allow it to happen again. I suited up for war and brought arms. My mouth was my sword and my heart was the annihilator. Throughout middle and high school, I picked fights with boys to prove that I was stronger, smarter, and tougher. I played the dozens until I saw tears in a niggas' eyes. I focused on my books and didn't allow my crushes to go too much beyond that.

I hung out with boys for the most part; taught to always keep the enemy close. Learn their thoughts. Study their moves. Use it against them in times of war. By age 18, I was one of the only virgins left in my neighborhood, lonely, but content. College came. Hormones churned. My body said "yes," my sword shouted "no." My sexuality won, but I intentionally left the emotional shit in the cellar, deep where no one could access it, not even me. I became sexualized vermin, caring none about men, more about self-gratification. Then the nightmares came.

The first year that I became sexually active, I began having recurrent dreams about my father. In these episodes, my father killed me several times by injecting me with the AIDS virus, shooting me in the heart at a noisy racetrack, and by raping me until I passed out. I woke up in cold sweats screaming for salvation and begging to be forgiven by my precious daddy. I thought these dreams meant that he had been right all along. I had turned into a stupid, good-for-nothing sperm receptacle, as most of my father's women had been (in his eyes), and as he promised I would be. I began to resent men even more because I felt so powerless and dehumanized. Maintaining a relationship was like keeping a candle lit in an ice storm. The closer they came to my heart, the more venom I spit, hoping to kill my vulnerability. I hadn't spoken to my father in years and felt if he didn't give a damn, how could anyone else? I decided to close the pleasure chest and took a vow of celibacy until I could figure things out.

What I realized was that in my rebellion and rejection of my father's ways, I had become his protégé. It was my way or no way, just like Charlie. I reveled in calling myself a female pimp and went so far as to found a "pimp club" among my women friends.

They took it as a joke, but I was serious as a crackhead looking for a television set to sell. I had relationships for sex and didn't have a concept of love, all tricks that I learned from Mr. Charlie himself. I said "I love you" because it was the lady-like thing to do and I treated men like refuse to be burned. The worse I treated them, the better I felt, until the guilt set in. Then I cut them loose. No tears. No drama. Charlie couldn't have done it better or with more ease. My relationships became power and control battles. This was the same dynamic that my father had with his women and later, with me. I have since learned that no one wins in a war.

Men are not objects for me to conquer. All men are not dogs. Women are not trinkets to be played with. And as women, we do not have to stoop below ourselves because our hearts have been broken. I have played the role of dog, bitch, pimp, and warrior as a defense mechanism and survivor of childhood trauma. My daddy broke my heart at a very young age, and it has taken years for me to reconcile that. Whether or not my father and I ever get back to our original place of love is unimportant.

However, I know now that I am in control of my actions and that getting to a place of vulnerability and trust is a good thing, not one to run away from. I have learned to hold my partner with both hands, loving him as my husband, not as a reflection of my father. I have learned to love myself, not as daddy's little girl, but as an intelligent, capable, tender, and affectionate woman. I love my father unconditionally for whom he is and understand that he is the person that he is because of what he didn't get from his own parents. I will be the one to break the cycle of dysfunctional relationships in our family and lead by example. Maybe one day my father will look up and realize that a woman ain't a bad thing to be and that with love, pimping ain't necessary.

To Err is Human. To Forgive, Divine.

*story contains some Bajan dialect

- Jacqueline Olurin

Daddy I know that you showed me love and my childhood was great, but for the longest time I harbored a bit of anger towards you. I can remember early in my childhood when you cheated on my mother. I didnâ't know that they had a name for your behavior until I was of age. Didnâ't you know that I was a little girl who loved my mother? Why did you put me in the middle of your dysfunction or I should say unhealthy relationships. What I am trying to say is, you exercised your manhood, your power over me, over my mother, and over your lover just to achieve an orgasm. No you didnâ't rape me physically, but emotionally I felt raped.

Daddy I canâ't forget your disrespectful ways. I was only eight-years-old when you sent me down the road to call Miss Barbara. It was early one morning; Mama was still at work. I didnâ't know what the meeting would be about, but my instincts told me that I was wrong for going to get Miss Barbara. I looked up to you; I worshipped you and would do anything for you. I guess, as Freud would put it, I was in my Electra stage of development.

The morning was cool; the breeze from the Caribbean Sea was brushing my face with a gentle whisper and a hint of fury. I didnâ't know what to make of the morning, but one thing that was for sure, it had an eerie feeling. I was in the middle of a scheme that was not of my design. I was my motherâ's betrayer and a co-conspirator. I was traipsing off to get Miss Barbara to come see you. I remember the laughter of many "Miss Barbaraâ's" only with a different name.

I remember as I stood on the outside of the many locked doors that something was not quite right. My mother was at work and you were with another woman. I eventually, freed myself. I told my mother what was going on. My mother was no fool, she knew.

I grew up with ambivalent feelings towards you daddy. I know deep in the recesses of my mind that my inability to sustain relationships had something to do with the way you had power over women and mainly my mother. I also look at men with a jaundice eye and refuse to be domineered or be their toy.

The final blow came at age 33, when I learned from you that you had children from two of the "Miss Barbaraâ's." How in the hell did Mama put up with your shit was beyond my comprehension? Her only explanation was, "I stayed because of you kids."

Life has a way of greeting one with the same medicine; the old adage, "What goes around comes around." I was ten-years-old the time daddy left the Island to come to America. Mama was by her lonesome. Because of my earlier work, fetching women for daddy, I thought why not fetch a man for mama. I saw an electrician who had a lovely gold tooth. That style of tooth was the norm and represented being of class. This gentleman came to the house to fix some light fixtures. I brought him a glass of freshly squeezed limeade. West Indians used more lime than lemons.

I could tell he liked my mother. He kept smiling. I canâ't tell where I saw him, but I told him my mother missed him and would like to see him. They began a friendship. Daddy caught wind in America and snuck back to Jamaica like a thief in the night. He and mama had harsh words. I felt guilty all the way around, for hurting my father, my mother, and her lover. I loved all three. The man was good to us, unlike my fatherâ's lovers who stole my fatherâ's love.

In making amends daddy, I love you and my love grew stronger for you when I saw you get on your knees and admit the wrongs you had done to my mother all in the name of "growing up." I forgave you more when you got a phone call 30 years later from my motherâ's ex-lover saying he needed some money for an operation and you gave it to him. I didnâ't understand why you did it, until you told me in coming back to America you had no money. Mama asked this man for the money enabling you to come back to America and start a new life for my mom, sister, and myself. In growing up, I now realize that life carries its own absurdities, and there are more questions than answers.

Anthony Keith Reily

- LaShaun Moore

I haven't written anything,
Spoken anything,
Thought anything about you
Since you've been dead.
It's been years, actually.
There are only two vivid memories
That I have of you.
I was young, maybe two,
And we lived on Young Street
In a flat, I think.
The roof was leaky.
There was a garbage can that caught the raindrops.
The raindrops kept time to the hits
You put on Mama's pretty face.
Snot-nosed Mickey Mouse (I called him that because I ripped off his nose
in anger)
Was there with me behind the garbage can, crying.
Crying like Mama cried.
When you finally came out of the bedroom,
Mama ran into the bathroom,
And I snuggled closer to snot-nosed Mickey.
I remember feeling violent as a baby.
I remember never wanting to see you 20 years later
In my boyfriend's eyes
His eyes looked like yours.
I remember hate.
I remember that you put that there.
And I remember that I loved you,
As I loved him—the boyfriend—Q was his name.
I remember ten years after that incident with Mama,
You showed up on my grandmother's doorstep.
You looked dingy,
Like snot-nosed Mickey.

MY SOUL TO HIS SPIRIT

Your nose was ugly.
Your coat was dirty.
You looked like a bum.
You asked if a girl named LaShaun lived there.
I told you that she was me.
You told me that YOU were my father
And I heard raindrops hit garbage cans and ran.
And hid.
And shortly after that incident you were in a coffin,
Leaving me wondering,
How you could love me and hurt my Mama like you did.
How you could look into my sister's face that looks like yours
And show up
Dirty,
Like snot-nosed Mickey and be hateful.
I remember hating my mother
For not telling me more about you until you were dead.
Still, I needed to write this poem to you:

Daddy,
Your blood runs in my veins.
Beautiful, brown blood like your skin.
I wear your smile beautifully.
I wore your rage just as easily.
I was once quick tempered as you were.
I am passionate for my causes,
As you were passionate for your violence.
I am confident,
As I believe you were in your youth.
I am charismatic.
I love hard.
And that is why I don't want to let your passion
Die in me.
I don't want to let you go.
I am sorry that you hurt my mother.
I am sorry that your life and death leaves an emptiness
In my sister's soul that she can't quench.
But, I am not sorry that I love you.
Not sorry that there is nothing else that I ever need to remember about
you,

Except that you are in my veins.
Mother made me utter something to you
When we visited your coffin.
Now at 25,
I finally believe those words.
I want you to know,
Wherever you are,
That I turned out all right.
I am brilliant.
I am not callused.
I don't get as angry as I once did.
I am more forgiving.
I am able to love.
And it is because you and Mama's blood consumes me.

Daddy,
In my quest for freedom,
For validity,
For liberation,
I needed to take the first step, which is simply this:
Despite the fucked up person you became,
I am proud you did something right when you made me.
I am proud to be your daughter.
You are forgiven.
Rest in Peace.

Father Found

- Jacquelin S. McCord

*"Therefore, if any man be in Christ, he is a new creature: old
things are passed away; behold, all things are become new. And
all things are of God, who hath reconciled us to himself by Jesus
Christ, and hath given to us the ministry of reconciliation.*
-II Corinthians 5: 17-18

I was driving along the expressway listening to the radio broadcast of the
Promise Keepers Rally at the stadium. Reverend Raleigh Washington
was speaking. He was talking about reconciliation: "Reconciliation with
God, with our wives, between the races of people, and between father and
son," he said. He asked the fathers who had brought their sons with them
to come out of their seats and stand together in front of the main stage.
There they would pray together and tell their sons that they loved them.
I heard the great rustling of noise as the fathers and sons began to move
forward as they had been instructed.

I put my thoughts aside and began listening to the program again.
The radio commentator described the scene for his listeners. "The fathers
are coming with their sons," he said. "Some are carrying their sons, some
are coming arm and arm, and some are hugging in front of the stage; many
of them are holding their sons and crying together as they pray together."
Afterward, the announcer conducted a few interviews as they returned to
their seats. The experiences they shared were moving and powerful. Their
stories were of heartbreak, recovery, reconciliation, and love. Tears began
to trickle down my cheeks. "Hmm" I thought, "I can't remember ever telling my father I loved him, or him telling me that he loved me for that matter." I had never even thought about it until now. Sure there were Father's
Day and Christmas cards signed "with love."

However, what in reality did that mean? Most people sign their
cards with expressions of "love," without any real thought. The more I
listened, the more the tears began to flow. I had to pull over, because I
couldn't see and didn't want to get into an accident. I began to sob uncontrollably as I allowed myself to touch the pain I had never heretofore
addressed. Like the fatherless lion cub Simba in *The Lion King*, my heart
cried out, "Daddy, where were you?" Where were you when I needed you

to read a story to me and tuck me in at night? Where were you when the neighborhood kids tried to set up a fight between me and another girl? I was so scared, but I talked my way out of it. I ran home and cried myself to sleep. Where were you when a neighbor down the street lured me into his house and then tried to rape me? I had to scream and fight my way out of there, but I escaped with my virginity intact. I didn't tell anyone, because after all, I was in the man's house.

I tried to regain my composure and I felt a little embarrassed by the stares of the passing motorists. "I needed to get myself together," I thought. "If I keep this up somebody will call the police and they will think I am crazy." My father did not play a major role in my life or my siblings' lives. He moved in and out of the house until he moved out permanently and my parents divorced. For the most part, I had forgiven him for leaving us a long time ago. Although we had a relationship, it was superficial. It was not like that of a father and daughter. Rather, it was more like an uncle-niece relationship.

Finally, I pulled myself together, wiped the tears from my eyes and got back on the expressway. At the time the program aired, I had planned a trip to visit him in two weeks. I realized then that it was no accident that I was hearing this program, rather it was ordained by God. Reverend Washington's message was gnawing at my heart. I knew in my heart that the purpose of the trip was to tell my father that I loved him. I knew what I had to do, but I wasn't sure I felt comfortable doing it.

The day for my departure came too quickly. I was traveling by bus which would take about 18 hours to get there. So I would have a long time to think about what I was going to say. My sister, who was the second oldest, was born when I was two-years-old. I don't think I had ever had a one-on-one experience with him since her birth. I was a little uneasy about this week long visit. Our previous encounters didn't require much effort. They were generally family gatherings and centered on a holiday or some other special event like a wedding or picnic. These meetings were with other people and didn't last for more than several hours. At that time we also lived in the same state. Now, we both had moved from New York—he was in North Carolina and I lived in Illinois. This time it was different, I was actually going to spend five days with my father. We would be sleeping under the same roof, having breakfast, lunch, and dinner together. The visit was also different because I had a mission/purpose and there was no getting around that.

The visit was a little awkward for us at first. We beganwith the small talk; the run down of the family list and updates on who is doing what and where. The silence came and the TV was immediately turned on. The basketball game helped to break the ice. I was very athletic and although not very good, I had tried my hand at basketball, softball, and volleyball. I also watch a variety of professional sports on TV, so I could hold my own in sports conversation. From that moment on, the rest of the visit was great as have been the subsequent visits. I was truly my daddy's daughter. We stayed up late watching movies, eating ice cream, and drinking soda pop.

Here I was a full-grown woman and very much in touch with the child within me. David Bradshaw, in his book *Family*, says that the presence of the man in the family causes children to feel safe, secure, and protected. In my daddy's house, that's how I felt—safe, secure, and protected. I helped him do the work in his garden and other projects he had to do around the house.

The visit was over much too quickly, each moment was to be savored. We were standing in the station waiting for the bus to come. Still, I had not done the deed for which I had purposed in my heart to do. "The time went so fast," I thought. The opportunity never seemed to present itself and to say it now would seem almost frivolous. The bus pulled up and the Holy Spirit seemed to be whispering in my ear, "Say it, say it!" He handed the bus driver my bags and then we hugged good-bye. I said, "I had a great time dad, thanks for everything. I love you." He hugged me back and answered, "I love you too, Sugar."

He Was Always There

- Nadine McIlwain

I left his apartment feeling somewhat satisfied with the results of today's visit. Finally, the shoe was on the other foot, as they say. Instead of him teaching me, I taught my father a thing or two. Now he can access the web, chat, send and receive emails. He even has his own password and email address. Miracles never cease.

My friends respond with muted laughter every time I start a sentence with, "My dad said..." or "My dad did...In one hour." "Your dad taught you to how to type in one hour" they would say. "Yes!" I emphatically replied. We started with the home keys and then he would give me a word including a different letter of alphabet and showed me which finger to use. I couldn't convince them or Miss Kelly, my typing teacher, that 60 minutes after I sat down in front of his old Royal typewriter I was touch-typing. But I knew the truth. That is not all I learned from my father. I can make minor electrical repairs to clocks, radios, and electric fans. I have replaced wall sockets, rewired lamps, and installed dimmers on the switches in the family room. Thanks dad.

My girlfriends heard the stories, or more correctly, the adventures I shared with him, many times over the years. Those, with whom I shared a friendship with since jump rope days, knew. For the others, there was always the hint of disbelief, as they listened, challenging only the most hard to swallow parts. Every word was true; and try hard as I could to convince them, in the end, it really didn't matter what they believed. I was the eyewitness. Like when I told them we had the very first television in the city of Canton, Ohio, because my dad made it. With his own hands, as a project for broadcast school while a student at Kent State University, my father soldered together wires and plugged in enough tubes, to produce a black and white moving version of Howdy Dowdy on a three-inch screen. "Suuuurrrrrre," they said.

When I told my friend Sherry that my father was taking my sister and me to see Millie Jackson, she said there was no way she would go see a Millie Jackson show with her father. I had to remind her that we were closer to 40 than 14 and she said that it didn't make any difference, Millie Jackson was beyond risqué. I told dad what Sherry said and he brought her a ticket also. The four of us had a ball. Dad laughed out loud as we ogled, with mouths wide open, and watched Millie (did she really touch him there) getting up close and personal with a front seat male patron. Or when, and this is my favorite story, dad and I were having a conversation about how my husband and I could afford to send our daughter to college. Dad simply said, "Give her $20.00 and if she really wants to go, she'll go." That is when my girlfriends lost it. I admit, it sounds a little unbelievable—a college education for $20.00, but I knew of what he spoke.

I was 18 and just graduated 21 out of a class of 400. My grades got me scholarships totaling $400.00 which I could access only upon acceptance and admittance into a college. I had dreams of Fisk, Tennessee State, or Howard. Totally out of the question, but I did dream. Although I seldom asked him for much, beyond the emotional support, wisdom, and love he freely gave, this one time, I needed money and my father was my last hope.

"Dad," I said. "Can you help me? I need money to go to college."

"Sure," he said, "I can give you some money."

Not sure he understood, I said, "I mean now. I need it right away, by Monday, or I will lose my scholarships. I can get a ride to your house if you can give me some money."

"All right," he said. "Come on up."

"Up" was Akron, Ohio a neighboring city and a 30-minute drive north. Traveling the highway in a boyfriend's car, I figured out my whole life. I would take my father's money and combine it with the scholarships to pay for my first semester at Malone College. With my father's help, I could get a college education and graduate. In four years, I would be a schoolteacher, something I wanted since the eighth grade.

We arrived at his home and he immediately began talking politics. After an hour of whether or not Kennedy was doing a good job, and what would happen to the country if Richard Nixon became president, it was time to leave. "Here," he said, opening his wallet and removing a $20.00 bill that he handed to me, "this is all I have." I said thank you, kissed him, and we left. I cried all the way home. My dream shattered. That was Sunday. On Monday, I took the $20.00 and paid the application fee to Malone College—exactly $20.00. Eight years later, after much hard work, I graduated. Dad was there. I taught American History for 20 years at Timken High School, where my father was the first African-American male graduate. My classes were real lively during presidential election years.

I shared the $20.00 story with my daughter the day she graduated from law school. She is quick and when I finished, she said, "Granddad gave you more than $20.00, he gave you all he had." Amen.

He was there, always there. It seems strange since I never lived under the same roof with my father, but he was always there—high school and college graduations. Weddings. The births of my daughter and son. Grandchildren's birthday parties. Christmas, Easter, Memorial Day, The Fourth of July, Labor Day, Thanksgiving. Family reunions. My husband's death. My son's college football games when my husband was no longer at my side. My mother's funeral. The day I was sworn in to serve as a member of Canton City Council. My retirement party. He was always there.

I saw him cry twice. The first time after the death of his mother, the woman he entrusted to raise my sister and me. My grandparents never locked their door so finding the door locked and nobody home was enough to bring tears to my father's eyes. The second time, it was my fault. I wanted to know, needed to know why he divorced my mother when I was only six-months-old. I had asked him this same question many times before and he replied that business between a husband and wife, was just that—end of discussion.

I asked him again after mom died and he said if I were his wife he would tell me, since a man owed that explanation only to his wife. Maybe the illness caused him to relent, but the breakdown I witnessed as he recalled events long ago suppressed, made me want to hold and comfort him as I would a child. Words and tears flowed together in one torrent, washing away the soil of the past for both him and me. He needed to tell me and I needed to hear.

I was caught off guard, but not surprised, when he refused to accept the cancer diagnosis. "I DON'T HAVE CANCER," he shouted to doctors, nurses and me when we tried to convince him otherwise. He underwent the chemotherapy for six months and radiation therapy for one month, but it was for a blood clot, he said. And when he had enough, he thanked the doctors for curing him and said he didn't need any more treatments of any kind. That is when I brought him the computer and taught him how to go on line.

His eighty-second birthday was February 8, 2004. I looked into my father's eyes and I saw the strong defiant man inside, a little less strong, a little more defiant. I pray he is right. I pray that those insatiable tumors are not living like parasites off the nutrients of his body. I pray that the invisible cancer is not hiding in shadows ready to visibly claim his spirit. "I DON'T HAVE CANCER!" he exclaims, but sometimes he needs my help to carry the groceries. "I DON'T HAVE CANCER!" he tells the grandchildren, but his back is not as straight, and when I remind him to stand tall, he does so for about a minute before returning to his bowed state. "I DON'T HAVE CANCER!" he says, refusing to hold the railing when he walks up the stairs, because holding is a sign of weakness. I worry that he will fall.

His eyes are not as clear, but he only needs glasses to read, he reminds me. I want to help him, you know, do as much as I can while I can. He lets me clean his apartment without protest, but objects if I want to help him balance his checking account. "Okay," I say, knowing his mind is as sharp and focused as ever. Leaving his apartment, I think, no monuments will be erected to honor him. No building will bear his name after he is gone. His life will not be written about in news stories. Yet, they should be, because he defines the word father. I turned to kiss him good-bye.

"Are you going to vote for George Bush?" he asks.

Dust From the Past: Let it Settle

- Joann Potts

Growing up without my natural father after age 11 was very painful, and for a long time, unforgivable. You see I had an uncle for nine years of my young life, who was my surrogate father until his death. He loved me as much or more than any natural father could love their own child. It was after I lost him that I began to yearn for my natural father.

At the age of two, I was taken from my mother and stepfather and delivered to my aunt and uncle's house to live until I was 21. Growing up under my aunt's roof and abiding by her stringent rules was no "crystal stair" for me. Her rules were very harsh and strict, and she had a temper as mean as a rottweiler at times. I survived the first nine years living with her, because my uncle covered me with all the love he could give, and took most of the abuse himself before he passed on. After his death, times got incredibly hard for me, because I had to live alone with my aunt and there was no one to turn to when the times got really tough. Those were the times that I wondered about my natural father and needed him the most. I used to think to myself, why didn't he come and take me away from all the abuse and cruelty of my aunt? He lived in Gary, Indiana, hundreds of miles away from Jackson, Mississippi. Many times, I found myself dreaming about him coming to get me to take me away from all the abuse.

Later on in life, I was told the real reason why I was taken to live with my aunt and uncle at the tender age of two. At that time, I was being physically abused by my stepfather, because he didn't want me. I was not his biological child; therefore, he would beat me when I would wet my pants, even though I was not potty-trained.

My stepfather had plotted to give me away to some strange woman. My grandmother learned of his abuse and insane plot, and rushed to rescue me. She took me away from my mother and stepfather. She later took me to her brother's house and asked if he and his wife would raise me. They agreed, because they had no children of their own.

It was extremely hard for me trying to survive under the tyranny of a brutal aunt. I withstood the beatings, because I had no one else. My great-grandmother would remind me that my uncle had left money in the bank for me to finish school, because education was a priority to her. It was her way of encouraging me to stay with my aunt for the benefits that lie ahead.

The physical beatings and verbal attacks were the hardest to endure at my young age. Today, it would definitely be called child abuse. Those were the times, when I would dream and pray for my natural father, the most. I wanted him, so badly, to come take me to live with him in Gary, but it never happened.

He didn't show up until I was 17-years-old and a senior in high school. I will never forget the first time he came to my aunt's house to meet me. I was surprised to see him. We went out to eat together and he visited me several times while he was in town. Even then, I had a strange and distant feeling towards him. I tried not to show it. I guess you could say I was glad to see my father for the first time in my life. I kept wondering why did it take so long? Where was he when I was suffering with polio? Where was he when I desperately needed a new pair of shoes? When I was being brutally beaten...where was he? I used to think to myself, if he couldn't come, why didn't he send his family to see about me? All of these anxieties and more lay dormant in my mind for years.

Today, 40 years later, we have a decent relationship. I call and visit him when I can. Although I still have some unanswered questions, it doesn't bother me as much now, because I feel I have made it through the troubling times of my childhood. Why bother stirring up the dust of the past—let it settle and stay settled.

I am not bitter towards my father. There are times I don't feel very comfortable, alone, in my father's presence when it's just the two of us together (maybe because we never bonded as father-daughter). He has made a few vague statements, trying to justify what happened in the past. I am still not sure that I understood them.

Maybe one day, I will share with him my concerns, then, maybe I won't. At this time in my life, I feel like "I made it through, why bother?" I love my father and always will. We frequently tell each other "I love you" and I am glad. I will continue to stay in touch with my father, as long as possible and maybe one day, I may gently share a few thoughts with him; if not, I will still love him, regardless.

Our Father Who Art in Heaven

- Jacqueline Ward

I spent the early part of my life traveling between Somerset, New Jersey where my paternal grandparents lived, and Greenville, Mississippi where my mama's people lived. During these formative years of my life, from 1958-1964, I actually never saw my father strike my mother, for that matter, cannot remember him ever striking us either. But he must have. He must have. What else could account for the sheer terror we felt every time he would enter the room? My mother would start to tremble if he called her name a certain way. My sister and I would sit transfixed on a couch or a chair, shaking so much, and on more than one occasion actually wetting ourselves when he was in one of his moods. Maybe he had lost at gambling or was unlucky with the ladies, I don't know. All I know is that I hated and feared him. And what other reason, aside from abuse of the worse kind, would send a mother out, abandoning husband and four small children, in the middle of the night under the pretense of going to a church revival.

Long before my mother left, my three sisters and I were estranged from our father. Even at the tender age of three or four, I refused to call him daddy or any other term of endearment. We all did, we called both our parents by their first names, Frances and Lee. One day Lee called us into the bedroom, "From this point on you will not call ya' mama by her first name. You will call her mother or mama. You will refer to me as your father." So from that day on, Frances became "mama" and Lee became our father literally as in "Our father, may we go out to play," or "Our father may we have another piece of chicken."

For as frightened as we were of him, this was our one little stroke of rebellion, and no matter how much he threatened and scowled, we called him "Our Father" with a capital O and F. He must have known that it was the one little thing that he had to leave us. He couldn't have known that we were plotting his demise in our tiny little heads had he tried to force us to call him anything else.

It was his "timely" death when he was 31 and I was ten, that I began the road of discovery of who my father really was. In fact, it was only after his death, at the hands of a fellow gambler, that I learned to love him. At the age of ten, the idea of continuing a relationship with my father, even though he was physically departed, seemed as natural and real as anything else between these worlds. I not only grew to love my father, but we began a journey of friendship, mutual respect, and admiration that would continue for the rest of our "lives."

It was only after his physical death, that my mother shared his story with us. Perhaps she too grew to understand and appreciate him more with the quantum gift of time and distance. I grew to see him not as innately evil but just a very angry black man with an explosive temper living in incendiary times.

A series of stories I never tired of hearing involved our travels through the South. A recurrent theme during our travels in the early 60s along the highways between Mississippi and New Jersey, were the stories of his refusal to adhere to the Jim Crow laws that still existed back in the early 60s. Back then, we had to carry a big container such as a coffee can in the car, so that the children could pee in it as we were not allowed in public restrooms unless they were marked "colored." Oftentimes there were no separate facilities just "white only" facilities. Sometimes my father would just say the hell with it and take us into the bathrooms anyway.

Another version of the story was how my mother would have to sit in the driver's seat sometimes with her foot on the gas peddle. Whether from frustration and anger or maybe just for the fun of it, my father would sometimes run into cafés and truck stops and demand to be served at the counter like everyone else. Most times people were so intimidated by him—he was a very big black man like the kind they draw on posters that they would serve him. Other times I guess the locals were feeling their "Wheaties" and would refuse him service. Well of course, Our Father would have to knock somebody out and we would then beat a hasty retreat. I remember his robust laughter as he ran out of the restaurants. I guess this was his way of proving that he was a man and alive. Not content to just exist, at 31 he seemed to thrive on adventure and controversy. Our Father was a man who loved to live on the edge.

Our Father also loved to gamble. His work schedule was erratic as he worked for his father who owned the local "colored" grocery store and radio and television repair shop. I am not exactly sure what it was that he did for my grandfather. I suppose that he helped out at the stores and occasionally helped him to manage some of the real estate my grandfather owned. Whatever he did must not have required too much effort because he was often at home, too often for my taste.

While my mother was busy bearing and rearing children, my father took it upon himself to educate me in the ways of academia and the world. After breakfast, which usually consisted of home made biscuits, oatmeal, and honey gathered straight from the bee's nest. He would school us.

A quick study and eager to learn my letters, this was the time when the two of us were the most simpatico. He enjoyed teaching and I loved learning. Afterwards during the warm months, I would either join my mother and two younger sisters for their mid-morning nap in the grass in the backyard or if invited, go wandering through the large wooded area behind our house with my father. One time he showed me how to build a grill using just bricks and pieces of stone and later that same day, he tried to teach me how to trap a rabbit. I was much better at catching rats and mice, but we didn't eat those. The two rabbits that he caught were skinned and roasted on our homemade grill. I remember sitting there picking at the rabbit thinking, "It doesn't taste like chicken to me."

We had plenty of time for mis-adventures between his work schedule and my being home schooled each day stretched interminably ahead of us. I am not sure that I appreciated the time then, but I do now, for as ambivalent as I was about my feelings about him, it is quite gratifying to be able to pass these tales on to my younger sisters who never really knew him.

During the winter of my tenth year, we learned to love each other. This relationship continued over a number of decades. Every decision that I made, I consulted him first. We would visit at night in my dreams. We would sit for hours fishing, or painting the rooms of our house or driving around the country. Sometimes we would spend the time just sitting, talking, and catching up.

The 20s were pretty rough for me. Unsure about the direction of my career, how I felt about family and marriage, I sort of drifted from one track to another. Finally ending up back in my original profession, working for one of my first bosses.

One day when my second child, my daughter, was about ten-months-old, and I had been with the company for about two and half years, I received a visit from one of my ancestors. It looked like my grandfather, but I wasn't sure. I just knew that it was one of my ancestors, a man in his early sixties or so. He simply said to me, "You were meant for greater things than this. You come from a long line of great people." Then all of a sudden we were by a great river with sunshine and pyramids in the background. Out of these pyramids, poured my ancestral line as long as the eyes could see, of beautiful and colorfully dressed people. People who had come before me and those that would come after me. This man proceeded to introduce me by name to the hundreds, if not thousands of family members. It seemed to go on for hours and he was very methodical about introducing them to me, each and every one by name. As he did, an instant picture of who they were, I mean who they really were on a soul level, flowed through me.

I put the vision behind me. About a year and a half later, the ancestor returned. This time he really did look like my grandfather, which puzzled me because, my grandfather was still alive. "Still here?" He asked with a little note of censure in his voice. And in a ripple, all the ancestors stood behind him, peering over his shoulder looking at me. It was very powerful and I realized that I needed to get out. It took awhile but finally in a leap of faith I left the job without any prospects. My spirit lifted immediately and all the demons that had plagued me drifted away, never to return. It was only much later that I recognized that ancestor. It was my father. You see my father died at the age of 31 when I was barely ten-years-old.

The conversations during my 20s, the walks in my teens, and the advice over the years had all been with a man in his early to mid thirties. I had fixed the ancestor who visited me at the age of early 60s; the age my father would be had he lived. No wonder he resembled my grandfather.

Daddy

- Charlene Hill

At 12-years-old, my parents separated for the last time. I remember standing in the airport. It seems we stood for eternity waiting. It was a sad moment.

As an adult, it occurred to me how little I knew about my dad. And so I wrote him a letter sharing this revelation. My sharing did not bring the relief for him that it brought for me. Instead, I heard through the family grapevine he felt hurt. I felt at a lost in terms of communicating the distance that made him more of a stranger to me than a beloved Father. Calling him "father" felt awkward as though I were forming my mouth to utter a foreign language. How could I help him to see it was not his character I was judging, but the lack that existed in our relationship? Our relationship plummeted into no contact.

This lack of relationship seemed fine to me. I reasoned that I would rather have no relationship than to have a pretentious relationship. I have never been able to embrace falsity and pretentiousness in my life. I can be lonely by myself so why participate in loneliness brought on by the company of another. In my own cowardice and inability to find and/or construct bridges to be in a relationship with my dad, I retreated.

I cannot recall how we reconnected. I know it was through no great effort of my own, but it happened. I am meeting my dad for the first time, and I find that he is not this large, luminous, and dark presence in my life. He is no longer bigger than life, but he is a part of my life. We laugh a lot. We plan our vacations at the same time so that we can see each other. I look forward to his phone calls. Our time together is sacred. We negotiate our needs as daughter and father.

I am finding my voice in his presence. I find myself, like a teenager, challenging him and grateful that he allows me to stretch my own wings. I am starting from the developmental space of saying goodbye in the airport. Though we are both opinionated, neither has to tower in the other person's presence. We are not alike, but we share some commonalities.

I have had to ask myself how much of what I perceived of my dad in the past was given to me through the pain of my mother. Since I did not know him, how did I paint the landscape? How much of my understanding was constrained by childhood memories and experiences? I have not relinquished the ambiguity of the past, but I am attempting in the present to revisit the past with my father. I need his help to live more fully in the present.

I have not found all of my voice, but I am taking steps in that direction. I still feel awkwardness when I address my father as "Dad" or end our conversation with, "I love you." In fact, I shudder as I consider what I must now share with my dad in order for our relationship to remain healthy and productive. I know that it requires risk on my part. However, I can tolerate the awkwardness because of our mutual relationship. I can venture out more because of the space we have built together. I also know and believe my father is open to the reconciliation process.

28 Years Later

- Melda Beaty

*J*ust left a po' white trash diner on the other side of the city where you seat yourself and the waitress takes your order after she crushes her third cancer stick. It wasn't my choice to come here, but as usual I gave in. The food is fast and cheap and the sounds of Bobby Blue Bland hovering overhead seem out of place. We sit in silence for a few minutes as he reads the menu. I pretend to show interest in the "Special of the Day" as my mind races to feed my mouth the appropriate words to begin the conversation.

"Daddy, I wanted us to meet because…"

"Y'all folks ready to order?" Her nicotine breath interrupts me.

"Patty melt and lemonade." My daddy immediately responds without even acknowledging that a lady *(me)* is sitting directly across from him.

I say somewhat apologetically for my father's lapse in courtesy, "Tuna melt and cream of broccoli soup please," but somehow I don't think she noticed or cared.

We say "thank you" in unison.

"Let's try this again," I say to myself as I fill my lungs with air. "Daddy, I wanted us to meet because I'm concerned about our relationship. I have wanted to talk to you about this for years, but…it just seems like we really *(I swallow to release the lump in my throat)* don't have a father-daughter relationship. I know that when I was away at school and work it was hard *(lying)*, but I'm here now and it seems that the only time we talk is about brother or money *(who gives a fuck?!)*. Brother has a problem, but it's not my problem *(sternly)*.

I love brother, but *(weak)*…it just seems like all the attention is on brother now *(fighting jealousy)* and I just want us to have a better relationship *(breathe)*. Significant things may be happening in my life soon and I want

you to be apart of them *(sincerely)*. It hurts me that we don't have a close relationship that's all *(exhausted)*."

His eyes jumped nervously from me, the ceiling, the lemonade, and back to me again, but when they landed on me they told me that he understood and didn't mean to disappoint me. So in his "this is the only way I know how to be a father" way, he just agreed with me, reflected on some things in the past about miscommunication with my mother and how he never knew what was going on with me *(as if calling me was not allowed)*. He talked about brother again with a few questions about my life thrown in for good measure.

See, daddy can't separate his world, the constant pursuit of the almighty dollar, and guilt from not being a better father-figure for brother, from what's going on in reality...true love and communication. Money and guilt are his only two frames of reference from which he lives, loves, and understands. I constantly tell myself that daddy's beginnings included alcoholism, physical and verbal abuse, below poverty living, and tea cakes for dinner. The love he did receive failed to teach him how to honor it by reciprocating it to others unconditionally—even his own children. I tell myself this when his void in my life gets too big for my heart to hold.

I see now that he will continue to live, love, and understand life this way, now and always. I guess I've known it, but secretly denied it. Does it mean he doesn't love me? No. Does he love me like I want him to? No. But he does love me and his willingness to meet me, his nervous laughter, and his wondering eyes, tell me that he would rather die before I stopped loving him.

So we sit eating our patty melts in a late night diner, 28 years later.

Deceased
GONE TOO SOON

"I cried uncontrollably and
knew the man I called 'daddy'
was not going to make it."

"...a black girl from Brooklyn...will simultaneously (and miraculously) bury her father
and celebrate her 18th birthday."

"We rocked and held each
other until the ambulance
came to take Daddy away."

CHAPTER VI

Deceased: GONE TOO SOON

f unerals can either unite or divide families. It is often a time of disclosure. Daughters who bury loving fathers will always have comforting memories that his love provided, but for daughters who bury a father that this life never afforded a relationship, his death offers little comfort coupled with unsettling memories. Whether he was an integral part of your life or not, every woman reaches what Reverend Fox calls a "place of reflection" in her life when she wonders "what would daddy say?" She refers to this period in a daughter's life as the "landmark ages" when she experiences marriage, children, career, buying her first piece of property, or divorce. Daughters of the deceased yearn for words of wisdom from their fathers especially during these critical times of reflection.

They have chosen the medium of words to define their emotions, ask their questions, make their peace, or just to say "thank you" to the man that gave them life when his life has ended. It is in their stories where her role as daughter transforms to the role of nurturer in his final hours. In order for her to experience true closure, the man that was once charged with being the protector, provider, and parent has to become friend.

Her journals, letters, and poems recount the entirety of her life, with or without, her father and how his death has given her voice. She engages in a conversation of two souls connecting on the spiritual.

Moving On

- Laylah Amatullah Barrayn

I'm not one who makes believes/I know that leaves are green/
they only turn to brown when autumn comes around
-Stevie Wonder, Visions

Raining on the day of someone's funeral is a confirmation that they have been granted heaven. It is an old southern saying you've heard from many family members. Aunt Grace and cousins are affirming this statement—while discussing the mysterious ways of the Lord—while adding the mayonnaise to the potato salad, covering chicken wings with flour, adding the pork to the greens. While spreading white icing onto your birthday cake, the twang of their southern voices fill with the hot air in the kitchen, and seeps under the door of your bedroom—like a chilling winter draft where you are silently lying there, on your bed, underneath light pink sheets, eyes closed, the souls of your feet facing the window, the soul of your being thanking the merciful God for the heavy rain this morning.

Above the tap-tap-tapping sound of rain hitting the window, and past the kitchen, in the living room is your step-mother: sitting on the couch, rocking back and forth, holding herself, humming *Amazing Grace*, in all black, already dressed for the funeral four hours away. You shift from lying on your back to your right side where you find yourself facing the huge mirror attached to the dresser. In the mirror is a black girl from Brooklyn who, today, will simultaneously (and miraculously) bury her father and celebrate her 18th birthday.

You pull the sheets tightly over your head, but in between the rhythmic beats of falling mercy you hear sounds making its way through the hallway, past the den. It is the sound of your brother dragging his boots across old wooden floors on the back porch. Thumbs in his jeans, head hanging low.

Pacing back and fourth and back again to have a seat on the bench behind him. He extends his ebony-amber arms across the back of the bench. His eyes fill will sadness; his head falls back.

The sound of the straw mat scratching against the floor as in-coming relatives wipe their feet annoys you; lividly, you fling the sheets off your body and into the air. Entering from the front door, then through the living room and around the kitchen are the voices of distant relatives. You can identify them as such by their template funeral commentary—

"It's gonna be all right!"..."He wit the Lawd now!"..."He ain't suffering no mo!"

Now you're pacing, as your brother once was, up and down the length of the dresser, wondering if the man putting oranges in a plastic bag at the Piggly Wiggly yesterday was your father. He could not be dead, not your father; because after a life filled with hard times due to poverty and ignorance, lack of vision and self-esteem, racism, and constant neglect, the least you were due was a father. You rationalize with yourself—index finger between your teeth, gazing at nothing.

When it's raining, down south at least, there is no noise in the house; everyone is quiet and all the electricity is off, TVs and radios. You know this rule, but when the stereo in the corner comes into your view, it politely suggests that you turn it on. You venture over there and press down on the play button. Michael Jackson commences to sing. "Let me show you/ let me show you the way to go...," and you begin to move. First you get the hip-hop-head-club-nod going, then your foot taps along with Tito's pulsating bass, and then, aw sookie sookie now, your black-girl hips come swaying into the groove, signifying the beginning of official gettin' down. And you're just dancing and its all good, because your daddy just can't be dead. God just would not let that happen. It is a party up in here, you silently declare.

You hustle your way to the door, lock it, and turn Michael all the way up to the max; "I don't know anything/ but that's something I do know/ I know/ I know...." You begin to releve, plie, chaine, turn pirouette style, tendu, and pas de chat; your room becomes Ms. Daiter's dance studio at Martin Luther King High. The class is going across the floor while wearing leotards. Ms. Daiter keeps the beat for the class with claps. You hope she does not burn your ear off with yet another story about her former landlord—trumpeter extraordinaire Miles Davis. The music switches to a song called Baxabene Oxamu; Harlem, USA is now the spot. Miriam Makeda's hearty, beckoning voice fills the Apollo Theater as you and Joan rehearse for a show. Ba-da-ba one two three, kick flat turn, singing the steps, and dancing the steps with Joan. You are traveling.

You smoothly land on the stage of Aaron Davis Hall, dancing with Forces of Nature Dance Company at their anniversary gala. A big beautiful black man behind you beats the devil out a Djembe drum. Your feet barely touching the ground, executing steps your ancestors once did on the soil of the mother land, while skillfully dodging Diane's long dread locks. Dang, you're bad.

Heading down town to Studio 54, runnin' away with Earth Wind and Fire. All y'all getting, donned with hundreds of small round reflections from the hanging sphere disco lights. You, Alvin, Judy, Authur, Katherine, and your dad's over there rappin' with Donny and the bouncer; Roberta's talking to Marvin at the bar. Then someone knocks on the door. "What the heck?" You figure, why be stingy with the party? You open the door to find the one and only, the hip-hop Prince of Darkness, Big Daddy Kane. The DJ spins that mellow Herb Alpert tune called *Rise*, the one with the engrossing trumpet flow, the one that caught Puffy's ear. Kane grabs the mic and flows over the track with sexual fervor.

Daddy and you have a seat in the VIP room. "Daddy," you say touching his hand. "You're not even dead. We went through all that trouble with the funeral, and everyone was so sad." You two locked eyes and he was silent. You and your father got on the bus and headed home. When your stop came, you both got off. And instead of walking with you, he remained. "Come on daddy," you wined. He stood in back drop of the dawn indigo sky and slowly waved goodbye. And that's when you knew this shit was for real.

You wake up on the floor with a bloody nose. Michael is no longer singing the soundtrack to your mental vision soliloquy. You unlock the door to go to the bathroom to clean your face. Your family is standing in front of your door with a confused look. Granddad asks if you're all right. You respond, "Yes," and head to the bathroom. The shower does not cool you off. Instead, the water engulfing your body reminds you of your father's arms that held you tight when he hugged you. The puddle of water at the bottom of the tub seems like the puddle of piss your father lied in after falling out of his bed at the hospital. The nurses there witness death everyday and are still not humbled. They spoke rough to him, and acted as if he was well and healthy and not dying from AIDS. Those arms that once assembled complicated toys, were now riddled with track marks and on the left arm, where the IV ran, would be the very last syringe to pierce through that beautiful black skin.

The limousines accompanied by the two Mayesville police cars, arrived outside the house. You sat in the last row, on the right side, your stepmother and brother on that same row. You ride slowly through Mayesville, pass the big white plantation house, with the wrap-around porch and the confederate flag hanging from the terrace, looking like it's playing possum. It had stopped raining by this time. Black girls wearing mini skirts and halter-tops pose on street corners; voluntarily scantily clad. Street corners where their great-great-great-grandmother stood— involuntarily—scantily clad-—on an auction block, soon becoming someone's chattel. You hated the south. It reeked of slavery.

The thought of having funerals never made sense to you. The person never looked the same as you remember them. Your father lied there, defeated, in a casket—a man who once walked down the block, with tremendous confidence, as if he owned both sides of the street. Upon laying your eyes upon your father, you feel the rage inside of you, pulsating upwards from your feet nearing the back of your knees. You are being destroyed. The rage, hate, and anguish battle in your soul. You can feel the fight in your groin, merging as they force themselves upward through your trembling stomach. You squint your eyes. This mixture of hate and fear moves upwards jabbing, and scratching, scorching your esophagus as heartburn does. It lumps in your throat, and you let out a long sigh, but the fight for your mind does not stop there. The rage infiltrates your sinuses and you become nauseous and lightheaded. Your eyes swell with tears, giving back the life and moisture to the layers of your dried out eyeballs. Hot teardrops fall from your face and crash onto your cuffed hands. The hate and pain continue on the path of destruction. They take over your brain, sending sharp pains back and forth across your skull like a guerrilla tennis match. The pain consumes your body, and with each wail your brother belts out, one degree of your security is depleted.

Then the metamorphosis begins; from daddy's girl to defensive woman. Standing over the coffin, taking that last look at him before they seal it tight, you make a promise to yourself to always fight to kill, to love, to survive. To always, no matter what the circumstances, surface as the victor with torch in hand.

But the void dad left was never filled, although you tried with Ozzie, Rick, Khiry and others. You still search the faces of medium-build, dark complexioned black men shopping at the Sharper Image with you as you absentmindedly shop for a Fathers' Day gift.

You visit your fathers, grandmother, aunt, cousin and other relatives' grave in that small spooky town in South Carolina three years later. After rubbing the soil of your father's grave in between your index and thumb, trying to become one again, you then realize that dad is closer to you that he has ever been. His spirit transcending the physical being and is every which way you turn. You run through the cemetery, feeling the wind on your skin, hugging father again.

Selected Journal Entries of Jacinta V. White

- Jacinta V. White

It is difficult to put into words my relationship with my father. None seem to adequately describe its depth and breadth. We knew what we had was special. I was told he saw it the moment I came from my mother's womb. I believe I felt it while I was still in it. So when I saw him take his last breath from suffering a massive heart attack, my life turned upside down. Here are journal entries that cast a blue spotlight on our journey together, and my journey through valleys of healing.

Wednesday, January 24, 1996, 9:30 p.m. Detroit, MI

My dad is so crazy. He just came in my room trying to dance like Michael Jackson. I wonder if your soul-mate can be your father? I mean, we know each other and understand each other like crazy. It's wild how identical we are. He's good for me and I'm good for him. I thank God that He gave me William Milton White, Sr. to be my father. Thinking about having someone else as a father is depressing.

Easter Sunday, April 7, 1996, 7:09 p.m. Detroit, MI

I am making myself write, because I've been putting it off for a month now. On Saturday, March 2nd around 3:00 p.m. dad passed. I still can't believe it. I used to think about his death occasionally to try and prepare myself, but nothing eases the pain or shock. I'm so confused about death—where he is actually, where is Heaven exactly; does he think about me, does he still love me? I often wish that when God took him that He had taken me too. I know I'm not ready to "leave," but it's too difficult to imagine living without dad...my soul-mate. I was so close to him through it all too: holding his hand, talking with him, praying for him—but death is stronger than my love.

Monday, May 5, 1998, 10:27 p.m. Atlanta, GA

I've tried recently to disconnect myself from dad—trying to be me, independently. You know, not wanting to feel that I'm worshipping or living for the dead. The Foundation that I've wanted to start in his memory lost its appeal to me because I felt it was too much "dad." I stopped wanting to remember him—thinking I could go on and have a fulfilling life. I want to be healthy and questioned dedicating my life to his memory, but what I'm now realizing is that the part of him I cut out of my life is the part of my spirit I need to help me to be happy. It's a matter of balance and keeping it all in the proper perspective. I felt I lost everything when dad took his last breath. A large part of me died when he died. Parts of me still die as I try to live without him. My fear is that what remains of us may not be enough for me to go on, and if it is enough, then will I truly be who God has created me to be? I've been making choices lately that go against me as my dad's child. Some positive, others destructive. I have to remember that I am mom and dad in one. I can't ignore either of their influences, nor the fact that my spirit is also a part of dad's spirit. He was all that is good to me. I must find that again and keep it close to my bosom. That doesn't make me weak or dependent, rather insightful. It's a long path to travel. Once again I got lost and confused, but thank God for Spirit which always guides and holds me even when I'm numb and oblivious.

Friday, March 3, 2000, 12:20 p.m. Atlanta, GA

Yesterday marked the 4th year of dad's passing. I had a good cry in the morning and most of the afternoon I was sad, but it got better. I didn't get that empty feeling in my gut this time when I cried, nor did I play through my mind what happened at that time four years ago.

Friday, March 8, 2002, 9:46 p.m. Atlanta, GA

My instant message buddy and I just got off. Wild, deep, crazy conversation as usual. He asked me what I would say if I was instant messaging my dad and I knew that was my last time communicating with him. The question caught me off guard, but I was more than eager to answer. In that moment I actually felt relieved as if I was really getting a chance to say "goodbye" to dad, as if he was actually going to read my message.

I printed the instant message, because I wanted to keep the words close. Here's what I wrote: "I would thank him for loving me and for making me feel like the most special daughter and friend in the world, for teaching me to be strong yet sensitive, for ALWAYS believing in me and giving me opportunities others dream about. I would tell him how I so love him: his strength yet gentleness, his integrity and faith, his commitment, his laughter and his hugs, being able to crawl up next to him in bed and listen to his heartbeat. I would let him know how very special he is to me and how I will never forget him."

Buddy's response was, "He knew all of that, and he would say to you, 'I hope I was the kind of father you could be proud of. I worked so hard, because I wanted you to have a better life than I. I'm sorry I can't be around for these years you need me most, but know that the same God who taught me will teach you. The same God that led me will lead you. The same God that held me up will hold you up. I love you J—and I know that we will meet again. Until then, live life to the fullest.'"

You can imagine how my tears were overflowing. I needed that, particularly then, in many ways. Trying to express the simple yet profound effect caused me to think of what dad would sometimes say, "Words are poor tools...."

I Never Got to Know Him

(ramblings about my dad, J. H. Pegues 1898-1991)

- Liberty R. O. Daniels

and the sad part is
that I never got to know him
he was a big part of my life
yet
he was never really apart of my life
how could this happen
we were a family of strangers
departing at different times
arriving at odd hours
dining together at first
then separately
as the emerson television set
wormed its way
into our daily routine
in the early 50s
causing friction in our lives
that was not present before
another vast silence
to outdo any of the other silences
we endured through the years
another escape
another reason not to interact
daddy was a tall slender man
6 foot 2
if he stood up straight
guess that's where I got my height
certainly didn't get it from that short woman
who called herself my mother
daddy swung his arms
from side to side
in front of him
when he walked

MY SOUL TO HIS SPIRIT

unlike most people
who swung theirs
back and forth
he walked everywhere
even to work
he spent 36 years
at the chevrolet manufacturing plant
and we never owned a car
until the year after he retired
and then he would refuse to ride in it
would rather walk instead
that 67 le sabre is still sitting in the garage
cream colored
with a black vinyl top
gold interior
still looking like new
still smelling like new
he never drove it
but he certainly took good care of it
he always carried money in his pocket
and paid his bills in person with cash
he never really cared about clothes
until the 70s
liked those leisure suits
could dress up
without really being dressed up
most of his clothes were brown or beige or gray
except that one navy blue suit
he always wore with those orangey brown pointed toe dress shoes
but on his birthday and holidays
he would let us venture some profound color
and style
into his wardrobe
he never bought anyone any presents
but was always the first one
to sit down in the living room
and let us lavish him with gifts
although he never served in the military
he came from a generation
that strongly believed in head coverings
when he was out and about
he always had on a top hat

usually a dress hat
and wore a trench coat year round
if he were just lounging around
his jacket would be topped off
with a cap
in the summertime
he always wore
that wide brimmed japanese straw hat
when he engaged in yard and garden work
he received a commendation
from the beautification committee
for the upkeep of his lawn
he was always so proud of that
especially after momma framed it
and kept it on display on the living room wall
he kept the lawns
at the properties they owned
in other neighborhoods
looking like his own
people always commented on how well kept
those properties were
especially the lawn
some folks even tried to hire him
as their gardener
or landscape artist
he always smelled of the freshly cut grass of summer
or of the newly shoveled snow of winter
or of old spice
a fragrance I always detested until he was gone
i slipped the remainder in the bottle in his bedroom into my purse
took it back home with me and wore it until it was gone
like him
kept the bottle for a long time after that
before I threw it out
daddy was a man who was in and out
of the hospital
for over four decades of my life
for one illness or another
one operation or another
bleeding ulcers
bowel obstructions
prostate cancer

he used to go into the kitchen
turn on the gas oven
just stand over the fire
letting the heat and warmth fill his face and chest
i never understood what that was about
he never said
and I was too timid to ask
he liked parched peanuts
and popcorn
gravy on everything
the friday night fights
his favorite sports were
baseball
basketball
football
hockey
and the prize fights
he was an avid lions, tigers, pistons, and generals fan
cassius clay was the only fighter who made him laugh
(he never accepted the name muhammad ali)
sports were his life
he saturated our lives with them
watching one game on TV
while listening to another game on the radio
i can still hear ernie harwell's voice
precisely pronouncing players names
like al kaline
like tony conigliaro
conigliaro
i'll never forget THAT name
conigliaro
had a nice ring to it
conigliaro
those athletes were all roomers in our house
taking my father away from us
that's why I hated them all
not the players
just the sports
daddy couldn't read
unless it was the sports section of the flint journal
would never let anyone else build a barbecue fire
went fishing every friday

no one could fry fish like he could
brought home live turkeys at thanksgiving
to roost in our coal filled basement
until thanksgiving eve
then he took them across the street
to the field where we burned our trash
wrung their necks
brought them back to momma to cook
for the holiday feast
we were appalled
my sister and I
although afraid of the turkeys in the basement
we considered them our pets
not dinner
daddy was ambulatory on the day he died
six days after his 93rd birthday
he wasn't feeling well that day
stayed in bed all morning
momma brought his lunch
sat with him while he ate
he told her he was sleepy
and was going to take a nap
she cleared away the lunch tray
and proceeded to wash the dishes
while she was in the kitchen
the angel of death visited his bedroom
i'm not sure what his death meant to anyone else
but for me
it was the end of an era
too late for me to get acquainted with my father
to learn anything about him
besides his name
(I will always be ashamed of that)
most of what I know about him
i learned from reading his obituary
somehow I always thought he was the oldest child
discovered he was the youngest of 11 children
born in 1898
to parents whose legacy was slavery
caused him to leave the cotton fields of mississippi
at the age of 13
and never set foot upon mississippi soil again

one by one
all of his sisters and brothers died
one by one
i missed ever meeting any of them
because they never came up here
and we never went down there
to me
those people were just letters in the mail ever so often
daddy had the smelliest farts
like somebody with a bad case of diarrhea
upon devouring lots of eggs, beans, sausage
after expelling gas
he would get up and leave the room
sneak out
those who stayed
literally subjected themselves to a gas chamber
as the odor filled the air
like concentrated insect fogger
one day
as he sat in the red fringe lounge chair
in the northwest corner
of the living room
with one leg dangling over the side
of the arm rest
he suddenly got up
went into the half bath
around the corner
in the hallway
i waited until I heard the door lock
then I crawled
over to the chair
on my knees
put my nose
directly in the middle
of the seat
and sniffed
i'm lucky I'm still alive

One Last I Love You

- Ieesha Hearne

*L*eaving Portland to set myself free from my significant other was the first time that I realized something was seriously wrong with my father. His personality went from being the life of the party to virtually not utter- ing a word. On many occasions, I was the only one who had noticed his sickness and it appalled me.

He had come from a family of five sisters and five brothers. When he was 16, he brought my Uncle Carl home whom his foster parents were abusing. Since my grandmother was already cooking for 11, one more mouth to feed would not have hurt. This was the type of man my father was; he always thought of others well-being before his own.

The only time I could bare to put up with them was on Easter and Mother's Day. They never cared for my Irish mother, and me. Since I am a product of my mother, comments like, "White girl" and, "Just because you are half-white doesn't make you better than us," were a constant. I learned to care for them less and less over the years. If a family could not accept a biracial person, how could the world?

My father and I never had a steady relationship in high school. He was a hardworking, kind man, and now that I think back, I do not know if our relationship was poor because we were too much alike or if he spoiled me rotten. In the beginning of 2000, whatever our differences were, I started to look past them. I constantly had these dreams about his funeral and him being dressed in a beautiful white suit. In my dreams the face was not visible, but consciously I knew the picture was him.

One morning while eating breakfast with my cousin Jerry, I told my father about my dreams. The look he gave me, lead me to believe that we both knew his secret.

He passed out at the steel mill and Dr. Monroe treated him like another African-American with high blood pressure. When he came home from the hospital his voice was faint. Every time that he spoke a word it seemed as though it was his last breath. I could not believe that he was released to go back to work, but before he returned to work we would have our last argument.

His attitude had evolved into the man my mother did not marry.

She had moved out of their bedroom and was thinking about a divorce. He and I argued because he apparently thought the fact that I did not have money for college next semester was funny. I did not think the matter at hand was funny, nor did I think his illness and the fact that my life had become being his personal nurse was funny either. I felt awful for screaming at him like I did, when I came to him to apologize he acknowledged that he was deathly ill. He confessed the reason why he crashed my car two months prior was because he blacked out.

I set up an appointment with his doctor a couple of days later and found myself dressing my father for the doctor. My mother of course thought that my dramatic personality had kicked in. Dr. Monroe gave my father an extra dosage of blood pressure medicine, set him up for an appointment with a psychiatrist and told my mother that it was all mental. Despite her reassurance from Dr. Monroe, I had a dreadful feeling that would not go away. That night I begged her to move into their bedroom with him. I felt it would be their last night as Jerry and Jane.

The next morning, I made breakfast for him as he went downstairs to watch TV. "Ieesha you need to go see what's wrong with your father," my mother screamed. The medicine Dr. Monroe prescribed sent him into convulsions and made him urinate on himself. I asked him if he would be okay and he answered "Yyyyyeeessss," as though he was a baby learning how to talk. We called the ambulance and my mother tenderly kissed my father's face.

For days the Neurology ICU did not know his diagnoses. His blood pressure was so high that an average person would have died on the spot. The MRI pictures, which were taken a month prior, showed major brain damage and seizures that weren't discovered earlier. The doctors met and decided the ICU at the University of Illinois Hospital would be best for him. One false move in lifting him into the helicopter would kill him.

On the final night, at Southlake Methodist, the nurse asked everyone to leave because his blood pressure was rising. Throughout his stay there, he did not have much movement and was unconscious ninety-eight percent of the time. As people were leaving the room, he lifted his hand up and pointed to me; grabbed my shirt and pulled me closer to his face and whispered, "I love you." I cried uncontrollably and knew the man I called "daddy" was not going to make it.

He arrived at the ICU in Ilinois. The staff was wonderful. At 4:00 a.m. Dr. Rabbin was sent to tell us about his brain surgery. My father was diagnosed with Cerebellar Ischemia. A condition in which an individual has enough high blood that it suffocates the brain. I kept thinking how young I was, how my father would never get to see my children or me fulfill my accomplishments.

In Illinois, he was not even able to open his eyes again. The doctors claimed he was not in pain. I told him repeatedly in his ear, "Thank you... even though you may have missed some of my games, my report card pickup, or sometimes my birthdays as some fathers do—I appreciate you." I would only get a few more hours to tell him the gratitude of a lifetime. At 5:35 a.m. February 23, 2000, the doctors said he had bled profusely and there was nothing they could do. He was the first patient at the university neurology intensive care unit to die in eight years. His family was all there and they gathered around his bed to sing him into heaven. As his flat line went from 100 to zero, I realized my life would never be the same without my daddy.

That moment was a moment of clarity. All the things that kept me from engaging with his family, at times, hating my interracial heritage and bickering over the silliest things became insignificant. I became proud of all the qualities of my father and sad that I did not have more than moments left to share with him.

Now, time has passed and sometimes I feel as though its all been a bad dream. I have continued to mature, develop, and evolve despite the death of my father. I have risen from bed everyday since his death, even though I haven't always wanted to. The world has continued with or without my loss. I have realized that you have to continue. It is just part of life. Understanding that eases my pain. Acknowledging some higher power empowers me and allows me to continue when all else fails. I now know my father's spirit was too strong to let a heartbeat stop it...in this life or the next.

Never Too Late

- Weena Stokes

I remember the day my father came back into my life. It was the day before senior prom, and I hadn't seen him since my mom packed up our things and moved us into a new home across town while he was out looking for work. I was eight then. Ten years later, I received a note in class that read, "You are wanted in the main office—your father is in the hospital." Immediately the tears welled up in my eyes. I hadn't seen nor heard from my father in over a decade, but the severity of that note awakened my feelings for him as if they had never lain dormant. My cousins, whom I remembered from childhood, were waiting to drive me to the hospital. As I sat numbly in the backseat of the car, they explained their reason for contacting me. My father was desperate to talk to me. Everything was so surreal at that moment. I was almost afraid to speak.

I arrived at the hospital to find my father lying in his bed surrounded by machines, tubes, and white bed linen. He was much darker than I remembered, and thinner too. His head was completely bald and signs of fatigue seemed to be permanently etched into his face. He took a moment to gather his thoughts. I don't know what I was expecting next, but I couldn't have guessed that my entire life was about to change.

My father informed me that he had been diagnosed with cancer. Because of his poor lifestyle and lack of insurance he had failed to get a check up until recently when the pain was too severe to ignore. The cancer had spread to five parts of his body already. He would begin chemotherapy within the next couple of days. Besides that, my father admitted that he had been living less than two blocks away from my current home, but never bothered to contact me until now. I didn't care about his excuses. The first news was enough to handle for now.

I struggled to bring the afternoon's events together in my mind. My father, whom I had not seen in over ten years, was back in my life just like that. I went home to my mom and siblings in a state of confusion. Needless to say they weren't much help at first. My older brother and sisters never liked my father. Besides suffering through our mother's divorce from their father, my father was the stereotypical stepdad to them. After losing his job, he became abusive and controlling. My mother enrolled in a nurse's aide program, got her license, and found a job. Secretly, she saved a portion of her check every month until she had enough money to put toward another home. My father had no idea of her plans. To this day, I try to imagine the look on my father's face after entering his half-empty home to find his wife, children, and their possessions gone.

My mother had long since forgiven my father for his abusive treatment toward us, but she was upset that he contacted me with such disheartening news. After all, we struggled to get along for many years after we left my dad. Money was tight and I was too young to understand everything that was happening. I became a bitter teenager who dreamed of one day becoming independent of everyone, including my family. The only thing that kept me grounded was my academic achievement. I was naturally gifted in school and my grades got me into a prestigious university. In light of the current situation, I planned to visit my father in the hospital while I was still in town, but I had no intentions of prolonging my college education.

I stopped by the hospital weekly to check on my father's progress. We began to talk about my future, my friends, and finally, my mom, and what happened a decade ago. I forgave my father for his mistakes. Seeing him in his current state of illness from the chemo, lacking the desire to eat and the ability to walk, it was hard to hold a grudge. I had been going to church faithfully for some time now and I knew that despite everything that had happened, he needed God most. My mom and siblings came around eventually. Getting over their initial reaction to his physical presence was difficult. My mom refused to come again, because it hurt her to see him this way. I understood, but continued to visit, though each visit got more personal, and each night it was harder for me to leave his side. He was becoming my father again, and in that same instance, he was slipping away. The chemo was ineffective and the doctors warned us that he didn't have much longer to live.

A month later, my father developed a severe infection. The doctors told him they needed to operate, but he had lost his will to fight. He refused the surgery and was moved to a hospice care facility. The first time I went to visit my father there I knew it would be my last. He was put in a small room, with no television. The only things present beside his bed were a touch lamp and a small radio, which we brought over from his other room. I took one final glance around the room only to find my senior picture tacked up by itself on a pegboard by the wall. At the sight of it, tears rushed to my eyes. I was emotionally spent. My father's body was free of tubes and machines. He was waiting to die. There was a morphine patch placed on his right shoulder to help suppress the pain. He was nearly unconscious from the strength of the medication. That day I sat with my father in silence, knowing that the end was near. I thought back on the day he re-entered my life and wondered why I had been given the opportunity to get to know him, only to have it stripped away again.

After hours of sitting, I woke my father to tell him goodbye. He squeezed my hand with what little strength he had and whispered, "I'm really sorry for my mistakes, Honey. I hope God has forgiven me just as you have." In minutes he was asleep again. I said a small prayer through my tears and left.

The past 12 weeks of long drawn-out visits and tear-stained pillows didn't prepare me well for my father's funeral. Though part of me felt relieved by the thought of him being out of his misery, I was struggling emotionally. My family thought that by attending his funeral they were lending me moral support, but I really didn't want them there. None of them, not even my mom, understood the man that I had come to know and love over the past nine months. I just wanted to be alone with him one last time, but when I was greeted at the funeral home by a multitude of sad faces I vaguely remembered, I knew that could never be. My mom and siblings found seats in the back, and I poised myself for that long walk to the front where my seat was reserved. As I took those first steps toward the casket, the heat from everyone's staring eyes could have burned through the skin on my face. I continued to walk until I reached the rope surrounding the casket. My aunt watched me closely as I focused my eyes on my father. The lifeless body that lay before me was enough to send me to my own grave. There my father laid, darkened skin, baldhead, almost an entire foot shorter than in real life. The cancer and treatment had robbed him of everything that I remembered being real about my dad. His casket was small enough for a child.

The tears rushed to my eyes, and my body rocked as if an emotional current was striking me. My aunt and cousin came to either side of me and led me to a seat directly in front of the casket. One of my parents was dead and the permanence of that reality was hitting me hard. I gazed around the room, desperately trying to bring familiar faces into focus. What I saw tortured my soul all the more. My favorite girl cousin on my late father's side was being comforted by my uncle, as was my male cousin's girlfriend by him. In fact, every woman in the room who was accompanied by a male was now being comforted in some way. It was at that moment that I realized the importance of having my father in my life all those years.

I stood up over his casket again, this time daring to lean against the rope and touch the metal sides. Their fathers were alive, and acting as fathers should, and mine was dead—lying before me in a casket that would soon be buried beneath ground never to be seen again. My emotions soared even higher as the feeling of being cheated out of the very thing that I wanted most in life washed over my being. There was nothing I could do. Nothing I could say.

I numbly walked back to my seat and sank into deep thought for the duration of the ceremony. When it was over, it was really over. I struggled through the repast and managed to say very little until we got to the gravesite. By then I had convinced myself that everything had a season—a time to live and a time to die. It was now my time to live, and learn from the mistakes I had already made in life. As the minister threw the first handful of dirt over my father's casket there were fresh tears falling from a few faces, but not mine. I had shed my last tear over his body. I was now ready to smile for his soul.

He Wasn't a Myth; He Was a Man: A Daughter's Revelation
- Vicki Meek

My father was a complex man. Although I guess I always knew this, it became abundantly clear to me how complex he was the older I got. When he died in 1995, I had been introduced to an entirely different man than the one I knew as a young child, a person that I never dreamed was in that tall handsome frame of a man's body. Stop. I should explain here that in truth my father died on May 24, 1982 the exact moment my mother's heart took its last beat. He, in that moment of her transcendence, had his spirit lifted with hers to the ancestor realm; his body just didn't follow. This marker in our family history served notice to all of us that life can be very short and although we have no control over when we'll be called to join our ancestors, we must control each moment we're alive. This is what my father always stressed as we were growing up and never did it have such meaning as when faced with my mother's untimely death. The interesting thing is although my father always espoused this philosophy, and in fact practiced it most of his life, he lost his grip on it when mom died. And that is when I began to catch the first glimpse of his complexity.

Like most African-American men who came of age in the Depression, my father had a clear sense of how America intended to mold him, and he wasn't having it! The social constricts that defined who an African-American man was in this country had no place in this African man's psyche.

He was the product of two very proud and distinguished African-American parents, and although times dictated otherwise, he knew he was destined to do great things. This sense of self is what I always viewed as his greatest strength and a trait I always tried to emulate. My father was his own man and no one could impose his or her will on him. This is who I thought my father was until May 24, 1982.

When my mother died, I suddenly was faced with the reality that childhood fantasies eventually get laced with reality. The myths I had created of who my father was were revealed in almost a cruel way. I was hit with the first blow as I was forced to look at the real "Dad" not the dad filtered through my mother's protective shield. The casual drinker was in fact an alcoholic who, as is often the case, was enabled by my mother's cloak of silence on this matter. With her, his alcoholism was usually held in check, without her it raged uncontrolled. The rock I knew as a child became a puddle of uncertain water with no boundaries to hold its shape. I was angry at first when I realized how much my mother hid from us until I realized that she did what any loving wife would do, she presented the very best of her mate at all times to whomever was interested in seeing him. Her children were dealt with in the same way so this should not have surprised me. As my father's life unraveled before my family's eyes, more and more myths were exploded and at some point, I began to assess my anger and deal with why it mattered so much to me that my father wasn't the mythic hero I had lived with for most of my life. All children eventually grow up to see their parents as they really are, apart from the creation of their childhood memories. I was no different.

But I think what disturbed me the most was how stupid I was to think that any man could be as perfect as I imagined my father to be. His frailties were human and simply put, not uncommon for a man of his time and placement in American history. That he managed to keep it all to-gether on the surface was admirable enough given the many traumas and disappointments I know he faced throughout his life.

I was 45-years-old when he died in 1995, and for the 13 years that he lived after my mother's death, I spent at least 12 of those battling with him over trivial things that were at best, "skin prickers," but certainly not "knife-to-the-heart" issues. But these were the things that kept exploding my myths, the lack of fiscal responsibility, and the inability to keep track of his business affairs, and the inability to face loneliness with more gracc. These were the things that placed me in the role of caretaker when I had no desire to be in that role. Not that my father ever became physically incapacitated, because he died not "being a burden to his kids" because he insisted on maintaining his independence, a state of being that was tantamount to being in heaven where he was concerned. But he became emotionally incapacitated which in some ways was worse for me to accept. I couldn't handle the deep sadness that engulfed my father when his mate, his friend, his lover, took her last breath. I wanted that pre-May 24, 1982 man to emerge from this tragedy and keep us all intact, but what I got was someone who only kept the wounds open by his very being. Every time I looked at him and his situation, I was reminded of my own deep, deep sadness and loss and I resented him for that.

The big, strong, self-confident, dynamic, African man had vanished

from the landscape of our family picture and what replaced him was unacceptable. No woman wants to admit that her father was "less than" and I was no exception, particularly given the unique position my father occupied in his community, that of the leader, the visionary, the architect of hope. I was furious that he could fall, no, dive so far off his pedestal, leaving me to struggle with his inadequacies.

Death, as it always does, forced me to reassess my relationship with my father as well as my need to hold on to childhood illusions. I was forced to reconcile my feelings of anger over things that I made about me but which in fact, were about my father and his struggle to maintain dignity in a world that insisted on stripping him of this God-given characteristic. What I, in my selfishness, saw as frailties were in fact signs of exhaustion from a man who spent the greater part of his life battling injustice and inhumanity towards oppressed people and who derived his strength to do so from the one group of people he knew would always adore him, his family. In coming to this realization, I grew up.

I have always prided myself on being a realist, a participant, not observer of life, a strong African woman made so primarily because of the positive and affirming relationship I shared with my father. The fact that my father illustrated all that was good in a man most of my life was a blessing. I now understand that many women cannot claim this.

But what I also now understand is that in showing me his frailties, my father helped me to better understand what my role as a mother of a son, and a sister of brothers, and a lover of African men must be to all of them. Even in death he continues to teach me; I have learned that being strong is often coupled with being weak; that loving someone mandates that at times you must create myths around that person, and that life has its own ways of testing your mettle, but that if your family is intact and the bonds secure, life's trials need not take you down. Yes, my father was a complex man, and it is only in his death that I fully appreciate that complexity.

Premonition

- Gloria Burgess

My father always said
he'd live to be a hundred.
In this I believed him
as in everything
else.

If he had to die
he only wanted to
with his boots on.
I'd picture him laid out
straight as a board
his feet sticking up
in his steel-toed shoes.

The last time he died
he died at home feet bare
as the day he was born.
He wasn't laid out
just plain worn out
from rage unignited
and generations
of mighty deaths.

A fisherman out of water
his hands hung from his wrists
like weights or oars.
He taught others to fish
without rod or net
and how to follow
dark to light
for he knew his way
by God and the stars.

He was a seer a netter
a climber a king
who'd made it by any measure.
Saw light in others
but not in himself. And I am
my father's daughter.

That Autumn Morning

- Gloria Burgess

Thinking of Robert Hayden
In memory of my father.
I thank God for his unconquerable soul.

I remember
You leaning
    for balance.
I remember
You before me,
    listing toward earth
      and heaven.

    Leaves dry
    raspy beneath our feet.
    Branches fallen,
    Chrysanthemums faded:
      musty memories,
      dying on mounds
      of autumn earth.
I remember
You steady
    speaking of plots
    as if you were talking about cars or trucks.
    How big (the funeral), what kind, how much.
    Not too fancy. Maple will do.
You lifted
    eased our burden
    even as, moment by moment,
    your body vanished into spirit.
I remember
You in your seasons
    and say a prayer:
    Rainmaker. Angel. Guardian.
I remember.

My Father, My Child

- Louise E. Mitchell

This is an emotional story of a strong and loving man, named Henry Alfred Mitchell who was my father, but before his death; he became my child.

He was born June 12, 1905. His mother and his siblings died when he was young, and his father for whom he was named, remarried. His relationship with his stepmother was not a loving one. She never encouraged him to do his best nor was she supportive of his desire to get an education. So at an early age he went to work to help support his family, while he continued to attend school. Her treatment of him was far different than that of her natural daughter who was the apple of her eye. I tell you this not so you feel sorry or sad for him, only so you would know how he began. In spite of his difficult childhood, he completed grade school and high school. He never let where he came from keep him from looking forward.

February 1929, he married Ethel Mae Crews; a commanding person who was a community activist; she raised money for the church as well as worked with other community organizations. After 29 years of marriage, Ethel died of breast cancer. She had a mastectomy as well as cobalt treatments. Henry and Ethel worked hard at saving her life but it was not to be; God called her home April 5, 1959.

Henry was devastated, however raising his children would make him gather himself since there were four still at home. He cut back on his outside activities, such as giving up his post as a state officer for the Masons, which he dearly loved, because it meant he would often have to travel for meetings and there would be no one at home for his children.

The younger children were ten and 11 years of age. He was determined to do all he could to see that they turned out to be the very best. As God would have it, Henry did a good job. His children turned out well. Kathryn spent many years in the book publishing industry. Violet became a commissioner for a New York City agency. Henry III became a career naval officer. James began as a professional football player then a successful automobile dealer, and of course, there's me, daddy's youngest girl. I own a small business, because my father told me I could do and be whatever I wanted.

During our years at home, he was still very involved in his community; PTA president, working in the church as a choir leader, even started the male choir, and served as trustee and treasurer of the church. He also became a mentor for a number of young men in the community that he met through the Masonic Lodge.

Soon changes in his health and mental state became apparent. This was the beginning of my father becoming my child. He had always been there for us and in the beginning you just don't want to notice the change. Daddy had always worked. He retired at age 65 and then went back to work. In essence he never retired. So when he talked about giving up his job, we made whatever provisions he needed so he could continue to have a reason to get up in the morning.

When daddy was 87 he became ill with a severe cold and bronchitis. He was still living alone and when we called he assured us he would soon be well. However what he was not telling us was that he was not eating or drinking much of anything. When we went home over the weekend he was sicker than we knew. We finally had to admit it was time for him to stop working and stay at home and that he needed someone to assist him with his day to day living.

Of course he did not want help from anyone. One will never know what an awesome road it is to travel when you take care of your parent(s). You can't know what it is unless you have had this experience. If this person was your child you would say "I'm supposed to do this, it is my child;" but when your parent(s) turn into son or daughter it takes a lot of time before you stop asking yourself, "Do you remember when...?"

I was daddy's point person, which meant that I was responsible to see that all was taken care of from coordinating the payments of his health care workers to having his medical needs handled.

This is when the fighting began. You fight with the doctors for the right medication. You fight with other office personnel to get them to treat him with respect because daddy would often say, "I'm a man and a very proud one." You fight with the magazine publishers and the credit card companies that send them things they didn't request, but they want to be paid regardless; with people that did work in the house that should not have been done; with people that you need to do small tasks which become a major problem; to changing payment plans so you can manage them better; to finally having everything changed to your address so you can take care of all the little things that they can no longer handle. You fight with your sisters and brothers, because you are responsible for getting things done and they are in denial about his present condition.

The amazing thing is with all the changes around him and all the battles fought for changes, the one thing is to have him feel that nothing has changed; that he is still in control, he is still the daddy. He was still my father, but he was no longer daddy.

Once he was my "son." My charge was to keep him well, happy, and alive. I tried my best, but daddy had plans of his own. He would not stay on this earth until he was 100 years of age as he so often said he would because three days after his 93rd birthday, he knew it was time to meet my mother again. He passed from this earth expectedly, because he knew it was time to go.

When my father-child left, it was a difficult task to stop the fight and to start to remember the time we spent together talking about my mother, how they met, and what fun they had together. I can remember he was always there for me. He raised me alone, teaching me valuable life lessons. He taught me how to cook and wash clothes so that I would be a self-sufficient adult. He was always in my life. Now I can remember that he loved me, not because he told me, but he was able to show me.

When I spoke at daddy's funeral the last thing I said to him was "we love daddy, but it is time to let go." Now that I can remember, I know I love him and I keep him with me so I can never let him go.

Because you loved me...

Crystal Renae Braboy

In loving memory of my Daddy
Elmore "Donnie" Braboy, Jr.
January 6, 1952- December 1, 2000
Your love sustains me daily...

It has been a little over a year now...I miss you so much. It seems like just yesterday you were giving me wet kisses and calling me Christmas. When you first passed, I began to think of all the things that you wouldn't be around to see happen in my life. I thought to myself—he won't get to see me graduate from college. He won't get to see me walk down the aisle. He won't ever know his grandchildren—I was crushed. I just knew my life would never be the same. My world no longer made sense. I thought, "You are half of me. Why would God take my father?" I didn't know which way to turn. But recently, I've realized that I can go on—I can make it—because you loved me....

Because you loved me, I am a stronger woman. I have no problem realizing my potential, because you always had faith in me. I will go on to be the classy, exquisite woman of color that you taught me to be. Having your love taught me that I could do everything and be anything I set my mind to be.

Because you loved me, I can love others. A father's love as strong as yours serves as an example of how to love others unconditionally. Your love taught me the power of forgiveness, the power of trust, and the power of prayer. So many nights I prayed to God to keep you safe. Your love taught me that loving unconditionally could be an exhilarating experience. I have learned to love with my whole heart because of you. And daddy, thank you for being the first man I ever loved. Nothing will ever replace that.

Because you loved me, I learned the appreciation of the little things in life. You taught me that a smile could speak a thousand words. Since you left me—I no longer take the little things for granted. The trees are fuller, flowers more beautiful, and the air more refreshing. Your eternal love has opened up my spirit. And since then, a peace like I've never known has taken over my body. That peace alone is the greatest gift your love has ever bestowed upon me.

Because you loved me, I can survive anything. Perseverance has been etched into my soul. No matter what trials come my way, I can handle them. I have learned that I inherited your amazing strength. I promise you that throughout my life, I will never forget anything I've learned from you, or learned observing you. In all endeavors, I will be the best—I will make you proud. As you guide me from our Father's palace—
I will achieve my destiny—all because you loved me....

Father's Day

- Jennifer Margaret Wilks

There was a time when I wasn't quite sure how to react upon entering a Hallmark store around Father's Day. I would go to buy cards for the various paternal figures in my life—the veterans such as my grandfather and the relative newcomers like my older brother—but I wouldn't buy a card for the person who seemed the most obvious recipient. I wouldn't buy a card for my father.

My father. Even now the words sound strangely formal. "Daddy" was how I referred to this remarkable man from the time I could talk until his death almost 16 years later. At 6'4½" he towered over most people. He was a full foot taller than my mom. Yet the imposing frame of the former college basketball player hid a gentle demeanor. That is not to imply that daddy never lost his temper or that my older brothers and I never got into trouble, but rather that, as the saying goes, such episodes were always tempered with the assurance that we were loved.

Daddy expressed a genuine, palpable interest in our lives. A day wouldn't pass without him inquiring about our time at school or work, and he followed through on these conversations with actions proving that he had actually listened. If I recommended a book from one of my classes, my dad would often read it whether they were young adult novels or political science texts, he took my suggestions seriously and readily discussed them with me.

Daddy was also fond of scattering notes of encouragement throughout the house: "Great catch!" for my brother's prize-winning fish, "Keep up the good work!" for my aced spelling test, but his interest far exceeded the basic parental desire to reinforce childhood accomplishments. When I couldn't find anyone to accompany me to Prince's Purple Rain concert, it was my father who volunteered to take me. Torn between amazed gratitude and preteen mortification, I ultimately refused, but I loved daddy for his offer all the same.

In what is perhaps homage to that never realized Prince excursion, my favorite memories of daddy are those, which recall his rich, musical voice. Many Saturday mornings, I awoke to the sound of laughter floating through the house as he and my Uncle Albert traded stories over the phone. At Christmas, whenever my dad and I heard The Temptations' *Silent Night* on the car radio, we turned the song into a duet, with daddy's deep baritone taking the lower notes in stride and my wobbly alto attempting the higher notes. After our efforts, I usually regained my breath just long enough to collapse into giggles. I still can't help but smile at the sight of the two of us singing along and what it must have presented to drivers who passed us on the road.

Those duets ended 11 years ago when daddy suddenly died days before Christmas. With clarity that time has yet to blur, I remember waking early one morning with the sense that something was terribly wrong. I stumbled into the hallway to find my brother Carl and my mother leaning over my father, trying to resuscitate him with the help of a 911 operator. My brother Eric pulled me from the spot where I had frozen and guided me to the living room. We rocked and held each other until the ambulance came to take daddy away. He died of an aneurysm en route to the hospital.

The next Father's Day, I was unsure what to do with the void left by my father's death. There was no card that I could buy to honor the most important father in my life—my own. Was I supposed to move celebrations of his memory back to Memorial Day or simply not hold them at all? I still wanted the world to know what a wonderful person daddy had been. Years later, when an unsuspecting coworker commented on my search for a Father's Day gift for my brother with, "Oh, I thought you were only supposed to get something for your dad," the grief I thought was behind me hurt more than ever. How could I answer her remark without conjuring depths of loss and love too overwhelming to navigate in the middle of a workday? I couldn't, and that incapacity both silenced and shamed me.

Yet with such lessons—and with time—have come new ways of remembering daddy's life. I can now make it through most of The Temptations' *Silent Night* without crying, and when I cannot, the drops that fall are not tears of sadness for my absent duet partner, but tears of joy for his continued spiritual presence. I hear daddy in the deep rumbles of laughter that erupt from my eight-year-old niece; it's almost uncanny how much she resembles someone she has never known. I see him in myself, now in graduate school, as I prepare to follow in his footsteps and become a college professor, and someday, I hope I'll feel his presence when my brother Carl takes my arm to walk me down the aisle.

So rather than dread the coming of Father's Day, I now embrace it and its rituals with the understanding that each memory of my dad, each moment shared with him, is more precious, more substantial, than any greeting card will ever be.

Cancer Dad

- Kimberly Rose

From my father, I inherited his mother's eyes, and yet I didn't see it coming. I don't think anyone did. I never imagined that my father, my provider and protector, the man who could discipline severely with the stinging clap of his voice alone, would look so small, weak, and in pain. In all of my 22 years, he had been the exact opposite. Now standing over him, facing this new reality, I grew up. In my own way, I wrapped my sick father up in my arms, and held him in a tight embrace that we had never before shared, but would not soon forget. I knew I'd see him strong again, and I did.

Cancer gave my father new life. Victory has that effect. Defeating a monster does wonders for the ego and replenishes the soul like sunshine in a blistery winter February. Cancer reincarnated my father, gave him new eyes, and for the first time I could see his soul.

I vividly recall the apex of our complex father-daughter tag team: Kindergarten, 1981. Every morning mommy would wake me for school before she left for work, and at 9:00 a.m. daddy would wake up and drive me around the corner to school. Then at twelve sharp, as sure as a father's pride, daddy's spotless white Buick LeSabre would be parked at the curb outside of school, with him inside tapping his fingers lightly on the steering wheel to the rhythm of soft rock tunes. His eyes were always hidden behind mirror-lens driving glasses.

"Your dad looks mean."

"Naw, he's just coooool."

After school we would bond over lunch. Hot dogs and fried eggs; or sardines sautéed in tomato and onion; or my favorite Vienna sausages straight out of the vacu-seal can, that daddy, once a renowned chef, would serve me without washing off the slimy mucous. He would make sure my cup of cherry Kool-Aid stayed full. And like any father and kid, we talked extensively about television.

Sadly, each passing year seemed to attach a more complex, impenetrable layer to our communication. As his youngest child, I outgrew the affection of cartoons and craved the attention and approval of my father. And yet growing up seemed mostly a fatherless affair. His presence in the house was characterized mostly by his absence. Daddies have to go to work, you see. Sometimes seven days a week, I learned. So when I encountered life lessons like fixing my own bike chain, bickering with my older siblings, battling my seven-times-tables, and learning how to set the mousetrap, mommy held jurisdiction over my world.

Most of my friends at school didn't know I had a dad. But I did. He was simply the silent partner of the parenthood, the focused venture capitalist who obsessively invested in our mortgage, groceries, educations, clothes and cable. The man with the disciplinary heavy hand. Daddy worked coarse calluses into his hands, but in my adolescent mind all I could appreciate, or perhaps resent, was his absent authority. He was little more than a shadow with a day job, a puzzling anomaly. A man more likely to render a butt whuppin' than a good night kiss.

At home daddy was normally a quiet guy, and I grew up recognizing the value of silence, but when he was among friends and colleagues, my dad turned into the life of the party. No voice was louder in his house, but his words sang like music to me. I danced to the melody of his laugh, a hearty boom of a cackle that was contagious and endearing. I was swept away in the animated spirit of the same father who worked over 60 hours a week and still forbid us from watching television with him on his days off.

My daddy's secret self helped me color in the mysterious silhouette of his silent parent persona, and I began to understand him. I had mistaken him for a miserable loner-laborer, who hid his emotions behind his trademark shades. But I saw through those mirror lenses into the eyes of an intelligent thinker and quiet observer. I saw me. The lines of communication to my father became clear and uncomplicated once I had learned his language. We developed a sophisticated and accurate system of written inquiries and memos, by which we would converse and keep in touch.

Hi Daddy. The last payment of the 5th grade class trip to Philadelphia is due next week Friday and me and Mommy didn't sell quite enough Katydids and designer wrapping paper this time, so I'm short about XX amount of dollars. Thanks!

I would simply post the invoice on the refrigerator, include the amount payable, and the billing date, which better not be less than a week away, and then wait. Sure enough, usually on the next payday there would be a stack of cash at the edge of my parents' dresser underneath last Christmas' unopened gift bottle of Old Spice to daddy from all the kids.

When I went off to college, I sent my father the most honest and direct note of my life in a thank you card. In it I told him how much it meant to me that he worked so hard, and that I realized that he sent me to a private university with the best Journalism department in the country—one that was far beyond our financial means—simply because I was worth it. And I told him I loved him. In all of the notes I had ever written to him, that was the first time I could remember writing those words.

And I was thoroughly convinced that my ink scribbles truly conveyed the depth of my heart's sincerity; more so than all the years' worth of Father's Day and Christmas gifts I ever gave him.

Two years later when his mother died in Jamaica, I remember actually telling daddy face to face for the first time that I loved him. When cancer joined our family one-year after that in 1999, I said it again so that I'd never regret it, even though I never believed for one second that he wouldn't survive it.

My father opted for surgery and subsequent treatments to handle his prostate cancer. He also decided to change his life. He quit smoking cold turkey after over 30 years. Cancer gave my father eyes to imagine the things that he could change.

Sadly, cancer came back twice and eventually claimed his last breath. In those last days my father was forced to listen. Listen to the steady bleeps of the medical machines that flanked his hospital bed. Listen for the heavy footsteps of the doctors and nurses monitoring his failing bodily functions. Listen to his children and grandchildren, wife, siblings, and friends hovering over him in sad laughter, solemn prayer, and sudden tears. He could no longer hide his emotions and reactions behind his mirror lens glasses. Could not watch his TV alone, without disruptions. Yet he still managed to communicate from the sick bed his lessons of hard work, family, and faith through his insistent reddening eyes. Admonished us for loud talking by shaking his foot and sighing, and said "I love you" with every courageous heave of his chest.

In the last days it was me who was absent mostly, a daughter simply unable to face her father's small, weak, pained existence. I spent those days working and praying. His last words to me were grunted through an oxygen mask.

"You didn't have to come today, Kim." We had an understanding. And I knew that was his way of not saying goodbye.

The Daughters
CONTRIBUTOR'S NOTES

Contributor's Notes

Opal Palmer Adisa

Opal's latest poetry collection is *Caribbean Passion*, Peepaltree Press, 2004. She has a forthcoming novel, *Painting Away Regrets*, and a short story collection, *Until Judgement Comes*. A mother of three, Adisa lives large and free and writes about love, passion, and those things that make life sing, dance, and rejoice.

Julie Amari-Bandele

Julie is a writer and e-book columnist.

Sharon R. Amos

Sharon is an Associate Professor of English at the Educational Opportunity Center and a doctoral student at the University at Buffalo. This year marks the 20th anniversary of her father, John Carl Richardson's death. She refers to herself as "my father's daughter" and relies on his spirit.

Adina Jordan Andrews

Adina has worked in a variety of student services roles at Northwestern University for over 20 years and is currently Manager of Student Financial Services. Her parents have been married for 56 years and she has been privileged to observe their love affair. She resides in the Bronzeville community in Chicago with her husband.

Avotcja

Avotcja is a poet/musician/photographer. She is the Founder & Co-Director of The Clean Scene Theater Project/Proyecto Teatral De La Escena Sobria. She teaches poetry, creative writing, music, and drama in public schools and is an Artist in Residence at Milestones Project & the Penal System. She is a proud and active member of DAMO (Disability Advocates of Minorities Organization) & the National Writers Union Local #3.

Laylah Amatullah Barrayn

Laylah hails from Brooklyn, New York. She studied at New York University and Cheikh Anta Diop University (Senegal); she now works as a journalist, photographer and essayist —her assignments have taken her around the globe to places like Jamaica, Malaysia, Morocco. Her photography was included in the Smithsonian photo anthology *BLACK: A Celebration of a Culture* edited by Deborah Willis.

Melda Beaty
Melda is the honored "mid-wife" for this labor of love, *My Soul to His Spirit*. She is a lover of the written word and all things beautifully creative. She is already underway on her next literary project, and has four other books written in her head and notes in journals. She shares this world with her loving husband, Peter, and her angel, Zora.

Meredith Bloedorn
Meredith was born in Milwaukee, Wisconsin and moved to New York City as a teenager. Her father was recently released from a long incarceration, and they have since enjoyed the simple pleasure of each other's company while walking down a street or sharing a meal. She is interested in the rights and concerns of families with incarcerated members, particularly the effect on children of incarcerated persons.

Chante` Bowns
Chante` is a sophomore in college majoring in English and Communications with a concentration in Professional Communications and Pre-Law. She is also an active member of King of Glory Church, located on the south side of Chicago. Writing has always been one of her strong points and when presented with the opportunity to write for this book as a junior in high school, she was both thrilled and honored.

Crystal Braboy
Crystal is a full-time college student, who interned for VIBE magazine. Penning this tribute to her father, whom she lost in December 2000, has helped her to speak to him in a way she was never able to when he was alive. The family-crowned "diva" enjoys singing, reading, and learning in her spare time.

Kathyrn Buford
Kathyn is a 19-year-old college student at the University of Illinois at Urbana-Champaign. She is more aware of how the past painful experiences, she once wanted to permanently erase, have helped shape the person she

is and will become. She likes the "new Kathyrn:" sensitive, thoughtful, and strong, and so does her daddy.

Gloria Burgess

Gloria's most recent book of poems, *The Open Door*, celebrates her deep connection to the oral tradition and evocative power of language. A Cave Canem Poetry Fellow, Gloria is also a senior leader and organizational consultant for a national foundation, an inspirational speaker, and an Affiliate Professor at the University of Washington. She lives with her daughter and husband in the Pacific Northwest.

Gabriella Caldwell-Miller

Gabriella is a Licensed Clinical Professional Christian Counselor in private practice, pursuing her doctoral degree in Human Services from Capella University. She and her husband, Rev. Aamon R. Miller, have two young daughters, Carolyn and Camryn. Gabriella still maintains a very special, loving relationship with her father and step-mother, John T. Caldwell and Valerie Caldwell, ESQ., who reside in Boston, Massachuettes.

Kimberly Cole

Kimberly's life mission is to help others realize greater visions for themselves. Her careers range from management to entrepreneurship. She and husband Vernon C. Cole III reside in Chicago.

Liberty R.O. Daniels

Liberty is a full-time poet, writer, performance artist, and the mother of teenagers 14 months apart. She is an advocate and active member of cultural and writing organizations, and the founding editor of *P.O.E.T.S. Newsletter*. In addition to being the Contest Coordinator for the Poetry Society of Michigan, she edits the quarterly newsletters for the Southeast Michigan Region of the International Women's Writing Guild and the Southeast Michigan Chapter of the National Writers Union.

Samaiya Ewing

Samaiya is a writer and performance poet in Chicago.

Tina Fakhrid-Deen

Tina directs a tutoring and mentoring program and is the Chicago Chapter Coordinator, for COLAGE (Children of Lesbians and Gays Everywhere). She is a published writer that loves to perform, travel, and direct plays in her spare time. She resides with her beautiful husband, Jashed and fabulous daughter, Khari.

Pamela Gilmore
Pam is following in the footsteps of her father. She is currently enrolled as a full-time student in the Mortuary Science program at Fayetteville Technical Community College. In her spare time she enjoys reading her favorite suspense novel or writing her upcoming suspense story.

Angela D. Gittens
Angela is a linguist, educator, and performing artist who enjoys sharing her crafts with children. She is fluent in six languages and a Ph.D. candidate researching and teaching the history of African Diasporic Performance at New York University. Angela resides with her husband and gives thanks for having witnessed true and unconditional love first-hand from (and between) her parents and in her family.

Tedella Gowans
Tedella is an adult instructor. She lives ten minutes from her mom and dad, and like her parents she was born in Texas and has a southern girl mentality. The inspiration for her submission was not difficult because in addition to her dad being her father, he is also her friend.

Ieesha Hearne
Ieesha is a student at Purdue University pursuing a degree in Communications. She is the recipient of the Women's Studies' Shirley Stanton Award. Her submission about her father gave her closure with her father's death and allowed her to express how people from multicultural backgrounds loose a piece of their identity when a certain culture is lost.

Charlene Hill
Charlene is an Associate Minister at Bryn Mawr Community Church. She is also a therapist/manager of the counseling program for Centers for New Horizons. She considers her calling helping others through restored relationships in self, God, and others.

Akua Lezli Hope
Akua is the first born of Albert and Hope, the third generation of her family in America and New York. Her first collection *EMBOUCHURE*, poems on jazz and other musics, won the Writers Digest Award in 1996. She has

been awarded fellowships from the National Endowment for the Arts, the New York Foundation for the Arts and the Ragdale Foundation.

Linda Susan Jackson

Linda Susan Jackson is the author of two chapbooks *Vitelline Blues* and *A History of Beauty.* Most recently her work has appeared in *Rivendell; Warpland; Brooklyn Review-21*; and *Brilliant Corners.* Her awards include a fellowship to Cave Canem and she teaches at Medgar Evers College/ CUNY.

Regina Jennings

Dr. Regina Jennings teaches creative writing poetry and literature courses in Africana Studies at Rutgers University. Her poetry books are *Midnight Morning Musings: Poems of an American African* (1998) and *Race, Rage, & Roses* (2004). Her forthcoming scholarly books are *The Malcolm X Muse in the Poetics of Haki Madhubuti* and *Poetry of the Panthers: Metaphors of Militancy.*

Denise L. Johnson, M.D.

Denise is Program Director of Melanoma and Associate Professor at Stanford Hospital and Clinics.

Kotanya Kimbrough

Kotanya is a teacher who has been writing short stories and poetry for children and adults for the last 13 years. She started writing novels within the last five. With two manuscripts completed, she is presently working on a third and compiling her children's poetry to create an anthology to be used in the classroom.

Nesheba Kittling

Nesheba is an associate with Baker & McKenzie. She wants to thank her brother, John, Jr., and her mother for fulfilling the "father" role in her life after her parents' divorce when she was 1 1/2. She would like to say to her father, "Forgiveness is the answer to the child's dream of a miracle by which what is broken is made whole again, what is soiled is made clean again."-Dag Hammarskjöld

Mae Koen

Mae has done support vocals for artists in numerous musical styles from blues greats Willie Dixon and Billy Branch to vocal crooners Miki Howard,

Phil Perry and Vesta Williams. Mae attributes VocalPoynt's, her jazz band, uniqueness to the ability to master all styles of music. Mae also plans to do a solo acapella project that will be in the vain of Bobby Mcferrin, while she is presently researching the many facets of African music and its merging together with music of the African Diaspora.

Toya Lay
Toya is pursuing her B.A. degree with plans on becoming a nurse. She inspires to write on a part-time basis and is an avid reader. She is the only girl in a family of six.

Gabrielle Lee
Gabby is a Sociology student at the University of Illinois.

Virginia K. Lee
Virginia is the Training/Head Start Licensing Coordinator at the NYC Dept. of Health & Mental Hygiene/Bureau of Day Care. She is also the Co-Coordinator of the Arts Ministry and Poet Laureate of Memorial Baptist Church in Harlem, NY. Her poems have appeared in several publications including *Soaring, African Voices, Wish Women* and the following anthologies: *Mourn Me In A Fed Dress* (2001), *Brothers and Others* (2002), *Warpland* (2003), and *Cave Canem* (2003).

Barbara Lewis
Barbara taught at New York University.

Michele Matthews
Michelle works full-time for a defense contractor. Her debut novel is entitled *Raymond's Daughters* (2004) and she has published other pieces in the *Journal of Intergroup Relations* and *How We Got Over...Testimones of Faith, Hope and Courage.* Her submission to *My Soul to His Spirit* was the inspiration for the novel *Raymond's Daughters.*

Jacqueline McCord
Jacqueline is the founder and CEO of T. Joy Andrea Publishers. She is the author of four books: *Miss America and the Silver Medal, A Molehill is a Mountain, When We Get Straight* (for children) and *Fur Coats in My Closet* (for adults). She is a member of the Apostolic Church of God and the Chicago Alumnae Chapter of Delta Sigma Theta Sorority, Inc.

Nadine McIlwain-Massey
Nadine is the co-author of *From Ghetto to God: The Incredible Journey of NFL Star Reggie Rucker.*

Vicki Meek
Vicki is a native of Philadelphia, Pennsylvania, and a nationally recognized artist who has exhibited widely. She writes cultural criticism for *Literafeelya*, an online art publication and *ARTLIES: A Texas Art Journal.* She is currently the Manager of the South Dallas Cultural Center in Dallas, Texas.

Louise E. Mitchell
Louise is the youngest daughter of the late Henry A. Mitchell. She is Vice President of Central Virginia Acceptance Corporation in Lynchburg, Virginia. This story was written out of a great love for her father and a thank you to him upon his passing on June 15, 1998.

LaShaun Moore
LaShaun has been performing spoken word poetry since 1996. She is an accomplished activist for such causes as "The Fight to Free Mumia" and "Stop the Violence," and recently organized a non-profit "Rage on the Page," which provides preventative alternatives to gun violence. Her poetry spans from topics of love, to gospel, to revolutionary mixed with soulful vocals, and she has had the opportunity to open for well known hip-hop acts including, The Roots, Mos Def, Dead Presidents, and Common.

Sandra Morris
Sandra is a freelance journalist/editor and award winning creative writer—hailing from Barbados.

Tawyeh Nishan-Do
Tawyeh is an aspiring screenwriter.

Nkiru Nso-Ani
Nkiru means "the best is yet to come." She is currently pursuing a B.A. in Accounting at American Intercontinental University. She lives with her "baby" (a two-year-old miniature schnauzer).

Jacqueline Olurin
Jacqueline is a nurse who writes stories and poetry.

Pam Osbey

Pam is the author of *Musings of a Mocha Sista, A Love Story,* and *Mahogany Passions.* She is the recent recipient of several poetry awards including the Gwendolyn Brooks Award presented by the Poetry Center of Chicago, and Most Popular Female Poet of the Year by Disilgold Literary Guild in New York City. She is currently working on her first novel which will be published in 2005.

Michelle Parrish

Michelle is the Founder of, and Coordinator for the ThickArt Collaborative, a Washington, DC based collective of female artist. When she is not painting, you can often find her volunteering in the community or working with organizations such as the Girls Scouts and the Family and Child Services of Washington, DC. You can view her work at www.thickart.com along with other members of the ThickArt Collaborative.

Suzetta M. Perkins

Suzetta is a Legal Research Assistant in the Office of the Chancellor at Fayetteville State University, which is also her alma mater. She is the mother of two grown children and one granddaughter. She is the co-founder of the Sistahs Book Club and has also completed two novels of which she hopes to have published soon.

JoAnn Potts

JoAnn is a Medical Technologist. She is the mother of the editor of *My Soul to His Spirit* and a proud grandmother. Her motto is "SAVED BY GRACE."

Imani Powell

Imani's writings have appeared in *Essence, Essence.com, The Source, Black Issues Book Review, Africana.com, Russell Simmon's One World Magazine* and in *Aunties, 35 Writers Celebrate Their Other Mother* by Ingrid Sturgis (Ballantine, 2004). Imani is co-founder of TEAMSexy, a web-based lifestyle design company, where she merges her love of food and design to create items that encourage all to Live Deliciously! She lives, creates and loves in New York with her partner in crime and design, Kaza Razat.

Kimberly Rose

Kimberly is a journalist, writer, editor, and young entrepreneur. With degrees in Broadcast Journalism and African American Studies from Syracuse University, the Rochester, NY native is co-founder of Echo Soul Publicity, Inc., a Harlem, NY-based Literary Publicity firm [www.EchoSoul. com]. Joslyn "Sonny" Rose died of complications from leukemia on September 3, 2004, just five days shy of his 61st birthday.

J. Victoria Sanders

Joshunda currently works for the San Francisco Chronicle as a features reporter. She has been a newspaper reporter for four years, and has also written for *Vibe, Popmatters.com, Africana.com* and *Horizon Magazine.* She's at work on a book of essays about the Boogie Down, the misadventures of black women dating in the 21st century and learning how to be freer.

Tauheedah Shakoor-Strong

Tauheedah is a Spiritual Life Coach. Her family remains a central inspirational force for exploring new frontiers of service in her life. Her upcoming book is *Flicker To A Flame: A Spiritual Journey Into Personal Power.*

Michelle R. Smith

Michelle is in her second year of English doctoral study at the University of Chicago, specializing in 20th century African American literature. She has a weblog called Safire (http://safire.typepad.com/safire/) and is working on her first novel. Her role models are her mother, Dr. Brenda R. Smith, poet Elizabeth Alexander, novelist Toni Morrison, and painter Frida Kahlo.

Weena Stokes

Weena is a native of Maywood, Illinois. She is presently working on her second Masters degree in Family Studies and training to become a Licensed Clinical Marriage and Family Therapist at the University of Maryland at College Park. Her future goals are to obtain her doctorate and work as a professor, practitioner, and novelist.

Mary Ruth Theodos

Mary Ruth lives with her husband and teaches kindergarten at a charter school that specializes in the arts. Mary Ruth's father is dying of cancer and she doesn't know how to contact him. Their last conversation was healthy and God continues to bring her peace about her father.

Tina Smith Walker

Tina currently teaches fourth grade at the Latin School of Chicago. She is a happily married mother of a six-year-old son, Ausar Nuari, and a one-year-old daughter, Kessa Meri. She is still working on that relationship with dad.

Jacqueline Ward

Jacqueline "JacQuie" is the proprietor of several micro-enterprises, including a knitting business with her 12-year-old daughter. She also teaches economics and business management full-time at a local university. Her family is one of a multitude of African-American families on the south side of Chicago who have banded together and elected to homeschool/unschool their children.

Jacinta V. White

Jacinta is the Founder of The William M. White, Sr. Foundation, Inc.—an organization in memory of her father that recognizes pastors by providing them with sabbaticals and other holistic programs. She is also a poet and published writer. Currently, she is the director of partnerships for a national nonprofit organization.

Jennifer Margaret Wilks

Jennifer is the daughter of Jacqueline Wilks and the late Dr. Carl Wilks. Jennifer lives in Austin, Texas, where she teaches English and African-American Studies at the University of Texas at Austin. She is currently at work on a book about African-American and French Caribbean modernist women writers.

Johannas Williams

Johannas attends Norfolk State University.

Niama Williams

Niama is a poet and scholar concerned with the survival of all creatures, and this orientation influences her teaching of literature, creative writing, and composition. She is a doctoral candidate in African American Studies at Temple University in Philadelphia, PA, who was born and raised in Los Angeles, California. She possesses degrees in comparative literature and professional writing from Occidental College and the University of Southern California, respectively.